Preparing White Teachers for Anti-Racist Education

"Straight to the point! Powerful, enlightening essays that urge teacher educators to do anti-racist teaching and to stop musing over what to do and how to do it. Each chapter gives reasons for why White teachers need anti-racist education."
—Carl A. Grant, *University of Wisconsin, Madison*

"This book is for any of us who refuse to retreat from the work of anti-racism in education and society. As teachers face increasingly complex needs of teaching all students, they deserve resources like this – grounded in research – to inform their practices in pursuit of equity."
—H. Richard Milner IV, *Vanderbilt University*

"This book will fill an often identified but rarely addressed scholarly gap. Significantly, it will help teacher educators to better prepare teachers. While many scholars and texts call for teachers to be prepared for racially diverse classrooms, few texts provide viable strategies for making this happen. Similarly, while many scholars and texts argue that preservice teachers must address their own assumptions and beliefs about racially diverse children, few texts describe how this might happen. In this text, readers will find both strategies for preparing teachers for racially diverse classrooms and essential practices for inviting novice educators to interrogate their assumptions. I highly recommend this book."
—Catherine Compton-Lilly, *University of South Carolina, Columbia*

"*Preparing White Teachers for Anti-Racist Education: Critical Reflection and Generativity for Transformative Praxis* is a timely, critical, and compelling book that addresses the need to rethink, reimagine, and restructure preservice and in-service teacher education to illuminate the anti-racist, educational dreams and possibilities educators can achieve."
—Nathaniel Bryan, *University of Texas at Austin*

"*Preparing White Teachers for Anti-Racist Education* is an essential academic resource that addresses the overwhelming Whiteness of the U.S. education system and the urgent need to prepare White teachers for anti-racist praxis. This insightful work provides critical reflection and practical strategies to restructure teacher education, fostering inclusive and equitable classrooms. It is a vital text for educators dedicated to transforming educational practices and advancing social justice."
—Nicholas D. Hartlep, *Berea College*

Katrina Liu • Michael K. Thomas
Richard Miller

Preparing White Teachers for Anti-Racist Education

Critical Reflection and Generativity for Transformative Praxis

Katrina Liu
Teaching and Learning
University of Nevada, Las Vegas
Las Vegas, NV, USA

Michael K. Thomas
University of Illinois Chicago
Chicago, IL, USA

Richard Miller
School of Music
University of Nevada, Las Vegas
Las Vegas, NV, USA

ISBN 978-3-031-73533-2   ISBN 978-3-031-73534-9   (eBook)
https://doi.org/10.1007/978-3-031-73534-9

This Palgrave Macmillan imprint is published by the registered company Springer Nature Switzerland AG.
The registered company address is: Gewerbestrasse 11, 6330 Cham, Switzerland

If disposing of this product, please recycle the paper.

This book is dedicated to
Ada Liu Miller
Kai Liu Miller
Rohany Nayan

FOREWORD

I first met the authors of this book in 2018, when I was on sabbatical from directing the Race, Inequality, and Language in Education (RILE) program at Stanford University. Throughout my career I have enjoyed working with like-minded collaborators who not only recognize the challenges of racial and economic disparities in U.S. schools but also understand that awareness is insufficient for transformation. Instead, we need clear goals, a plan of action to achieve those goals, and robust theories to craft responsive and flexible programs aimed at desired ends. Once we know that injustice exists, awareness must be followed by action to rectify injustices and strive for a better world. Over time, my combined efforts with the authors of this book in teaching, research, and writing have been a source of mutual fulfillment. It is therefore very gratifying to see this book come to fruition, encapsulating our shared dedication to addressing inequity in U.S. education. It stands as a testament to our collective resolve to make a difference.

Preparing White Teachers for Anti-Racist Education: Critical Reflection and Generativity for Transformative Praxis is an innovative book that is grounded in data. It is the fruit of more than a decade of research on the training and mentoring of preservice and novice teachers in anti-racist education. The research was conducted across three teacher education programs placing teachers in urban districts that ranged in size, with student and family populations varying in types of diversity, but always served by a majority White teacher corps. The authors use this research to make the case that, regardless of where teacher education is situated, teacher educators cannot assume their coursework and reflection projects are effectively preparing their future teachers to recognize opportunities and act in ways that advance equity and anti-racism in U.S. schools. This book makes clear that the stakes are not just high, but they are truly enormous. Preparing anti-racist teachers who can generate transformative change in the ways in which schools and schooling serve minoritized communities is one of the most important challenges facing teacher educators today.

It is clear from the data presented in this book that many White preservice teachers come into teacher education programs holding deficit-based 'habits of mind' toward minoritized students and communities. Consequently, preservice teachers' deficit mindsets lead to inequitable patterns of acting in their field experiences, often reinforced by their placement schools and mentor teachers. These habits of mind and patterns of acting, which actively traumatize minoritized students and their families, are perpetuated within institutions and propagated among K-12 students. These students learn early on that White students have the right to police minoritized students to preserve the privileges of Whiteness. This book shows that teacher education programs have not been successful in modifying White preservice teachers' habits of mind in no small part because too little attention has been paid to the preservice teachers' patterns of acting in the classroom, particularly in unscripted situations. This reality, coupled with the assessment focus of many preservice teacher reflection assignments, encourages a performative but ultimately "substance-less" approach to anti-racism and social justice in schools and schooling.

Fortunately, authors Liu, Thomas, and Miller do not limit themselves to pointing out the problems facing teacher educators who attempt to prepare anti-racist teachers. They go on to synthesize years of thinking on preparing critically reflective teachers who can generate transformative change. The authors then move on to develop a praxis approach to preparing anti-racist teachers that addresses both habits of mind (how teachers think about minoritized students and their communities) and patterns of acting (how teachers interact with minoritized students and their communities) in the context of racialized schools and schooling. The process the authors present employs a wide range of pedagogical tools—some of which may be familiar to the reader (such as reflective prompts, exercises, and opportunities for self-assessment) and others that may seem like new approaches to teacher education: but they all add crucial elements of serious engagement with minoritized communities. The result is a generative approach to teaching and teacher education based on the work of peers building anti-racist education together.

Finally, it needs to be said that we teacher educators know the issues, we know the patterns, and we may even know how to address many of them—but, as I clearly noted in Ball (2012), "to know is not enough." We need to know where we are going, we need to know how we plan to get there, and we need the will to act and complete the journey. This is the key lesson of *Preparing White Teachers for Anti-Racist Education*, one which the authors take seriously; and they provide us a framework and praxis for using the knowledge we have to generate transformative change in our schools and communities.

Stanford University   Arnetha F. Ball
Stanford, CA, USA
July 2024

ACKNOWLEDGMENTS

Every author knows that many people contribute to the final work in the readers' hands, whether by participating directly in the research and writing processes or by being part of the project indirectly by providing material, emotional, or moral support when the author most needs a friendly pat or a strong nudge. This book is no different in that regard, although perhaps a bit more complicated given that it has three authors rather than one, but one universal truth remains the same: any and all errors, misconceptions, and linguistic infelicities are the work of the authors alone, and not the responsibility of any of our supporters.

First, we would like to thank all the individuals who helped with the longitudinal research that forms the basis for this book, particularly our participating preservice teachers, mentor teachers, and their students, who welcomed us into their classrooms and their lives. We would also like to thank the principals and other school and district administrators whose agreement and support was crucial in maintaining access to their teachers and students over a period of years. Some of these relationships were created when the three of us were together at the University of Wisconsin, Madison, and so were facilitated by the teacher education faculty and staff at that university's College of Education; particular thanks here are due to Dr. Kenneth M. Zeichner, who has been supportive throughout the years. His impactful scholarship on critical reflection and community-centered teacher education (e.g., the new book titled *Communities: Keywords in Teacher Education*) has been an inspiration to our research and practice.

We would like to express our deep appreciation to Dr. Catherine Compton-Lilly, who supported the project from the beginning, providing research advice and methodological wisdom to multiple rounds of readings and comments to the early versions of the book. Her equity-oriented longitudinal studies of family literacy are a model of careful research and deep engagement to which we can only aspire.

The theoretical framework and program of action both have roots extending well back into our graduate student years, owing particular debt to Dr. Gloria Ladson-Billing and Dr. Carl A. Grant for the elucidation of Critical Race Theory in education and the various permutations of multicultural education. More recent scholars have also contributed mightily to the thinking and action described in this book, especially Dr. Rich Milner, whose numerous works on opportunity gaps, opportunity-centered teaching, and the most recent book, *The Race Card*, provide a timely example of how to handle the complexities of race and racism in US education with sophistication, elegance, and clarity. We thank him for his encouragement and support. We thank Dr. Nathaniel Bryan for many discussions in and out of AERA on the school-to-prison pipeline and the criminalization of Black boys. Above all, we must give special thanks to Dr. Arnetha F. Ball, who not only contributed important ideas such as generativity and generative change, but also has been one of our most consistent mentors and cheerleaders. It is no exaggeration to say that her brilliance, passion, and moral strength have propelled us to work to the highest possible standard. Without her, this book would not have come into being. Our special appreciation goes to Drs. Patricia Edwards, Xun Ge, Lin Goodwin, Danica Hays, Regina Murphy, Sharolyn Pollard-Durodola, Sharon Tettegah, and Jian Wang for their inspiration, encouragement, and mentoring.

Special thanks are due to the editorial staff at Palgrave Macmillan, particularly Executive Editor Milana Vernikova and Editorial Assistant Roberta Mistretta, who combine the patience of a saint with the tenacity of a bulldog. They know how much we appreciate both of these qualities, but here we wish to bring that knowledge to the larger public: they are wonderful editors who deserve all the praise we can heap upon them.

Finally, we would like to thank our families in Las Vegas, Chicago, New York, Wisconsin, Malaysia, and China for putting up with what turned out to be a larger book with a much longer gestation than originally planned. We had no right to expect patience for long hours of work both in the field and at our desks, or for the dinner table conversations that excited us far more than they excited our family members.

Portions of Chap. 2 were previously published in Liu, K., Miller, R., Ball, A.F. (2023). Teacher education for diverse learners. In: Tierney, R.J., Rizvi, F., Erkican, K. (Eds.), *International Encyclopedia of Education, vol. 5.* (pp. 356–367). Elsevier. Portions of Chap. 6 were previously published in Chap. 9 of Liu, K. (2020), *Critical reflection for transformative learning.* Springer.

The authors and publishers are grateful for permission to reproduce this content.

Contents

LIST OF FIGURES

LIST OF TABLES

CHAPTER 1

Educational Equity and the Teacher-Student Diversity Gap

Black people live and die every day under the burdens of a racism more insidious than the current virus that's also disproportionately killing us. And yet white people tend to take a slow route to meaningful activism, locked in familiar patterns, seemingly uninterested in really advancing progress. Theirs is still a world of signs and signaling, where actions like joining book clubs — often based in some "meaningfully curated" readings that are probably easy to name: "White Fragility," "How to Be an Anti-Racist," "Between the World and Me," maybe even "All About Love" — take precedence.
—Tre Johnson, "When black people are in pain, white people just join book clubs" (*The Washington Post*, June 11, 2020)

We began writing this book in a moment defined by two crises shaped by racism, one driving people into the streets and the other forcing them into their homes. The first was the years of targeted violence, intimidation, and systemic abuse of African Americans by the carceral state that culminated in police riots across the country, beginning with the murder of Michael Brown in Ferguson, Missouri. The collective response of the Black community to these police riots was to launch the Black Lives Matters movement, the mobilization of millions of people to demonstrate against both the systemic injustice meted out to people of color and the immunity granted to the agents of state violence against people of color. The second

K. Liu et al., *Preparing White Teachers for Anti-Racist Education*, https://doi.org/10.1007/978-3-031-73534-9_1

was the eruption of the COVID-19 pandemic, a global tragedy that disproportionately injured and killed Black, Indigenous, and Latinx people in US cities, intensified the over-disciplining of Black students in US schools, and prompted a huge increase in anti-Asian hate crimes in US communities. Neither crisis appeared out of thin air, and neither of them have disappeared, even though they have dropped out of sight in the mainstream media. Rather, these two crises were inextricably linked with their roots in the racism that has defined the United States as a nation of people, a system of institutions, and a practice of law since European colonization gave birth to a nation with genocide, slavery, and discrimination woven into its primordial tapestry.

Despite this legacy, the systemic bias and discrimination so crudely unveiled by the twin crises came as a surprise to many White Americans who were accustomed to think and act as if race played no part in their lives. One response by White Americans to the now-unavoidable reality of racism was a new round of 1960s-style consciousness-raising activities in "anti-racist" book clubs to "learn about and discuss" racism. But as Tre Johnson observed in his June 11, 2020 piece in *The Washington Post*, book clubs "are comfortable gatherings of friends who are unlikely to nudge one another to the places of discomfort that these books, at their best, demand."

As teacher educators, we find Johnson's description of "anti-racist" book clubs uncomfortably similar to how some teacher education programs prepare White teachers to teach students of color—focusing on revealing and talking about race and racism as abstract, distant problems. It is a perspective that is far less about taking immediate, concrete action to deal with these issues in the classroom on a daily basis. Making racism visible to White prospective teachers is undoubtedly an important task for teacher educators; in this book we, like so many before us, seek to provide some practical tools to bring proximity, visibility, and immediacy into being. But, as Johnson states,

> The right acknowledgment of black justice, humanity, freedom and happiness won't be found in your book clubs, protest signs, chalk talks or organizational statements. It will be found in your earnest willingness to dismantle systems that stand in our way — be they at your job, in your social network, your neighborhood associations, your family or your home. (The Washington Post, June 11, 2020)

Too often, teacher education programs teach the story of how racism "functioned" in the construction of American education as though it no longer exists and we are now presented with puzzling failures on the part of students of color that can be handled with one or two courses in multi-cultural education that offer White prospective teachers a few tips for dealing with "other people's children" (Delpit, 2006). The story of how White teachers perpetuate racism in American schools by failing to see racism while simultaneously benefiting from it is an important element of anti-racist teacher education. However, just as White book clubs are an incomplete answer to racism in broader society, teacher educators need to move beyond consciousness-raising sessions in teacher education courses and work with prospective teachers to critically analyze socially distorted assumptions about multi-marginalized students and implement transformative solutions to better support these students. The goal is not just to make White prospective teachers aware of the existence of racism from a detached, intellectual perspective, but to enable them to see it occurring right in front of them through the actions they themselves and their mentor teachers undertake. How might this insidious, persistent racism be cycled back, deconstructed, and ultimately replaced with more equitable, empowering, transformative, and nurturing practices and cultures in teacher education? It is with this goal in mind that we offer this book.

1.1   Educational Equity and the Diversity Gap: The Whiteness of Teacher Education

The need for anti-racist teacher education proceeds from the fundamental education debt (Ladson-Billings, 2006) and opportunity gaps (Milner, 2010, 2023) challenging educators in the United States to provide an effective and equitable education to students from all backgrounds (Ball & Forzani, 2009; Banks, 2006; Grant & Sleeter, 2007; Ladson-Billings, 2021). As of 2022, White students were 44% of the total US K-12 public school population. Students from other racial and ethnic backgrounds comprised more than 50% of the total student population, making White students the numerical minority with no single group in the majority (National Center for Education Statistics, 2024). It is the responsibility of our society and schools to promote high-quality and equitable education for all students no matter their positioning within systems of race, ethnicity, gender, socioeconomic status, sexual orientation, learning ability, religion, national origin, and intersectionality.

Compounding the reality of student demographic diversity, the nation's teaching force remains overwhelmingly White. In 2011, 86% of America's teachers were White (Feistritzer, 2011, p. 11). Twelve years later, the percentage of White teachers still remained 80% (National Center for Educational Statistics, 2023). Researchers have articulated a variety of problems inherited from the student-teacher diversity gap. At the same time, long-term social and political forces rooted in White supremacy have been hard at work reinforcing prejudice and discrimination in education as in all other sectors of American society, making the problem of educational inequity both intractable and urgent. Sleeter (2008) summarized a number of problems resulting from a primarily White teaching force. These include having difficulties in building constructive relationships with students of color, holding low expectations of students of color, interpreting students' lack of engagement as a lack of interest in learning, and blaming students' academic problems on an inability to learn (p. 559). These shocking yet ubiquitous practices reinforce a deficit view of minoritized students and their families (Valencia, 2010), removing the blame for low achievement—and the responsibility to address it—from schools and larger society. Further, Sleeter (2008) has pointed out that due to the combination of low expectations and cultural mismatch, White teachers are more likely to refer students of color to special education programs than White students and, conversely, are more likely to refer White students to gifted programs. This observation by Sleeter is confirmed by other scholars such as Milner (2010) who rightly criticized the opportunity gaps that exist between students of color and their White counterparts. Scholars have also noted discipline gaps between students of color and their counterparts due to a tenacious White supremacist ideology prevalent in the educational system, which affirms and maintains the ongoing construction of difference by the powerful to perpetuate the marginalization of the disenfranchised (Brown et al., 2009; Ladson-Billings & Donnor, 2008; Skiba et al., 2011).

A rising body of literature demonstrates that students of color are dehumanized, criminalized, and punished more harshly and more frequently than their White peers, even though they engage in similar behaviors (Basile et al., 2019; Bryan, 2017; Fadus et al., 2020; Hambacher, 2017; Owens & McLanahan, 2020; Wiley, 2021). In fact, the US Department of Education Office of Civil Rights (2023) states that "Black boys were more than two times more likely than White boys to receive out of school suspension or expulsion in K-12 public schools.... Black girls were nearly two times more likely…than White girls," estimating the total loss of more than two million school days over academic year 2020–2021 (p. 7). Basile et al. (2019) documented schools' hyper-policing of the bodies and behaviors of boys of color, routinely interrogating, controlling, and labeling them as "dangerous, violent, and truant" in a discourse that works to "support, justify, and reify criminalization as a normal, ordinary, and a necessary part of urban schooling" (p. 2). Black boys are treated as if they were older and less innocent than their White peers (Goff et al., 2014) and are even at times imagined to be "demons" (Bonilla & Rosa, 2015). Girls of color are generally perceived to be less innocent, stronger, and more dangerous than their White peers (Annamma et al., 2019; Pane & Rocco, 2014; Wun, 2014). They are also perceived as unfeminine, less "ladylike," and more aggressive (Morris & Perry, 2016; Zimmermann, 2018). This body of research shows that teachers, especially White teachers, often ground negative perceptions of students of color on a "racial grammar" (Bonilla-Silva, 2012, p. 1) held in common across American society. This racial grammar translates master narratives of students of color into "facts" that provide warrants for their punishment. The resulting criminalizing and dehumanizing practices have enormous long-term consequences for the lives of multi-minoritized students of color as they increase their contact with the juvenile justice system (Balfanz et al., 2015; Losen et al., 2015; Marchbanks III et al., 2015). Furthermore, White educators reinforce the "intergenerational lineage and socialization" (Bryan, 2017, p. 329) of criminalizing students of color by teaching White students to police their peers of color through their daily modeling; among those White students are the majority of America's future educators. Recognizing this intergenerational violence toward minoritized students of color and the distorted assumptions behind the violence is the first step for teachers and teacher educators to take in actively searching for transformative solutions with the ultimate goal of dismantling this miserable legacy—yet so far that recognition has not resulted in widespread anti-racist teaching and teacher education.

The persistent diversity gap has made the call for recruiting and preparing more teachers of color a perennial feature of education policy (Brown, 2014; Ingersoll et al., 2017; Liu & Ball, 2019; Villegas & Irvine, 2010), and prompted demands that White teachers be better prepared to teach a student population that will only become more diverse over time (Ladson-Billings & Ball, 2020; Sleeter, 2008; Zeichner et al., 2016). Teacher education programs have responded to this call by attempting to provide prospective teachers with pedagogical understanding and culturally relevant and sustaining teaching methodologies (Ladson-Billings, 1995; Paris, 2012; Paris & Ball, 2009; Sleeter, 2001; Sleeter et al., 2015). However, preparing White teachers to teach for equity is challenging, as their narrow framework of experience (Paine, 1990) makes it difficult for them to understand how racism operates in today's schools (Ladson-Billings, 2006; Utt & Tochluk, 2020). White prospective teachers typically harbor stereotypical beliefs about urban schools and communities developed over their years of "apprenticeship of observation" (Lortie, 1975, p. 61) that can manifest in destructive ways (Carter Andrews, 2009). Moreover, the Whiteness of the standard curriculum in teacher education limits the voices of people of color and their history of racialized experience while perpetuating White privilege and White supremacy (Bonilla-Silva, 2001; Picower & Kohli, 2017; Sleeter, 2017).

Research on White prospective teachers' beliefs and attitudes toward race since the 1990s has produced useful knowledge and practical principles for preparing future teachers for racially diverse schools (Ducey Jr., 2013; Jupp et al., 2019; McIntyre, 1997; Seattlage, 2011; Valli, 1995; Walker-Dalhouse & Dalhouse, 2006). For example, Jupp et al. (2019), in their analysis of 25 years of research on White teachers, identified numerous instances in which researchers note White teachers evading the recognition of race, White privilege, and Whiteness in general. In response, numerous strategies have been developed to try to overcome such "race-evasive" attitudes (Jupp et al., 2019), most of which rely on inculcating habits of reflection in prospective teachers, assessing any improvement through the evaluation of written artifacts collected in journals or ePortfolios. However, approaches emphasizing discussion and reflection related to racism do not guarantee that prospective teachers will actually take action to deal with racism in their communities, schools, and classrooms (Liu, 2015, 2020). Rather, teacher education programs that emphasize the production of written reflections and statements and use them for evaluation purposes, but limit classroom observation to short, prepared lessons, fail to support prospective teachers to take transformative actions that go beyond the abstract articulation of equity and social justice platitudes (Cochran-Smith et al., 2015; Liu, 2020; Thomas & Liu, 2012).

In short, encouraging (and studying) written reflections and prepared teaching demonstrations is not enough to prepare future teachers to construct and implement anti-racist teaching practices. Teacher educators need to examine prospective teachers' classroom actions (Capella-Santana,

2003; Howard, 2003; Sleeter, 2001), and must define teaching practices as "how to do the actual tasks of teaching," and not just "being engaged as reflective and inquiring professionals" (Cochran-Smith et al., 2015, p. 117). Moreover, although prospective teachers have been taught the basics of reflection in many teacher education programs, research shows that they distinctly lack *critical* reflection. This means going beyond a generic reporting of events in the classroom to engage in deeper intro-spection and examine the social and political contexts that underpin both prospective teachers' habits of mind and habitual actions (Liu, 2015; Liu, 2020; Liu & Ball, 2019; Thomas & Liu, 2012; Zeichner & Liston, 2013).

All of the above-mentioned problems with the conception and imple-mentation of reflective practice in teacher education programs have lim-ited the ability of teachers and teacher educators to develop effective anti-racist teaching and teacher education. Nevertheless, critical reflection within the framework of a social-cultural approach such as Critical Race Theory is necessary to address the operations of racism. This is, in part, because uncontested Whiteness pervades teacher education (Howard, 2003; Kohlii, 2008; Matias & Zembylas, 2014). Teacher educators reaf-firm Whiteness as the norm when they fail to engage their students in active participation in anti-racist teaching (Galman et al., 2010), or struc-ture their programs to avoid conversations about them (Pollock et al., 2010). These failures constitute engaging in "race-evasive" teacher educa-tion (Jupp et al., 2019). It is imperative that teacher educators find ways to leverage White prospective teachers' abstract grasp of race and racism in education and develop this into an active engagement with the daily reali-ties of lived racism, prompting critical reflection for transformative learn-ing (Liu, 2015, 2020; Mezirow, 1990, 2003). However, creating this linkage has yet to be adequately explored. In response to this need, this book examines prospective teachers' *habits of mind* (Mezirow, 1997) and *patterns of acting* (Mezirow, 2000) in dealing with racial issues, and what teacher educators can do to help prospective teachers critically analyze their habits of mind in order to foster transformation and generativity in their patterns of acting. We are guided by three overarching research questions:

1. What habits of mind regarding race and racism are evident in pro-spective teachers' reflective practice?
2. What patterns of acting regarding race and racism are evident in prospective teachers' classroom teaching?

3. What can teacher educators do to help prospective teachers critically analyze their habits of mind in order to foster transformation in their patterns of acting in their teaching practice toward anti-racist education?

1.2   HABITS OF MIND AND PATTERNS OF ACTING

During the Civil Rights movement of the 1960s and 1970s, African Americans demanded that society respond to their quest for "social, political, economic, and educational rights and possibilities that had been denied, lost and betrayed for more than three centuries" (Banks, 2013, p. 73). One outcome of this struggle was an effort to include the history and cultures of non-White America in school textbooks and curricula. Nevertheless, although the pioneers in researching and teaching non-White American history and culture were themselves members of those communities—from W.E.B. DuBois (1903) and Carter G. Woodson (1933) to Vine Deloria Jr. (1969), Sucheng Chan (1996), and Ronald Takaki (1998)—the overall effect of much of the curriculum and pedagogy in the ensuing multicultural education movement was limited to cultural enrichment for the dominant White majority. Since then, cultural difference theorists such as Ladson-Billings (1995, 1999) and Moll et al. (1992) have argued that more active inclusion in the pedagogy of the diverse cultures of marginalized groups should benefit all students, not just White ones. Cultural difference theory has produced multiple pedagogical approaches, including "culturally appropriate teaching" (Au & Jordan, 1981), "culturally congruent education" (Mohatt & Erickson, 1981), "equity pedagogy" (Banks & Banks, 1995), "culturally relevant" pedagogy (Ladson-Billings, 1995, 2014), "opportunity-centered teaching" (Milner, 2012, 2023), "culturally responsive teaching" (Gay, 2000), and most recently "culturally sustaining pedagogy" (Paris, 2012; Paris & Alim, 2017)—all of which are used to prepare White teachers to work with diverse student populations.

However, efforts to implement these approaches in teacher education have been repeatedly stymied by two primary factors: the *habits of mind* brought into teacher education programs by White prospective teachers (Case & Hemmings, 2005; Dedeoglu & Lamme, 2011; Dee & Henkin, 2002; Gainer & Larrotta, 2010; Jackson et al., 2016; Richardson, 1996); and the perpetuation of racist *patterns of acting* by in-service teachers and administrators (Blaisdell, 2016; Kohlii et al., 2017; Ladson-Billings, 2000). Habits of mind are "habitual ways of thinking, feeling and acting influenced by assumptions that constitute a set of codes…that may be cultural, social, educational, economic, political, or psychological" (Mezirow, 1997, p. 7). Prospective teachers have developed habits of mind regarding race, racism, and education both from their personal experiences, from larger society via the media, and of course from their apprenticeship of observation (Lortie, 1975) during their own schooling. However, when left undisturbed and unchallenged, habits of mind can become *toxic*, reproducing unconsidered assumptions grounded in broad social and political practices, including race, class, and gender. Milner (2023) provided a long list of "under(lie)ing conditions" that represent the enduring expression of racist habits of mind in the policies of schooling. Milner (2023) framed them as lies such as the "representation lie," the "Asian Model Minority lie," and the "achievement gap lie" underpinning our attitudes and pervading our collective culture (pp. 23–24).

In the context of racialized classrooms, the apprenticeship of observation reinforces White supremacy and hegemony through discriminatory, punitive actions on the part of White teachers against students of color. Bryan (2017) pointed out that these actions are observed and internalized by their White students who assume superiority over their peers of color and grow up to be White teachers in the classroom in an "intergenerational lineage and socialization" (p. 329). Research (e.g. Gao et al., 2019; Liu, 2020; Ray, 2022) provided examples of White students learning to police the boundaries of Whiteness by imitating their teachers, inflicting school-based intergenerational trauma on non-White students; we provide more such examples in this book.

Importantly, from Mezirow's (1990) point of view, habits of mind are not just an issue of "viewpoint" affecting how individuals understand and interpret the world. They also direct how people act in society. What Milner (2023) identified as "under(lie)ing conditions" (pp. 17–24) are based on systematically distorted assumptions about students and communities of color and lead to concrete oppression in schools and schooling. For example, the Asian model minority lie—the assumption that all Asian American students perform well in calculation-rich STEM disciplines—leads to the denigration of their ability in interpretive and expressive disciplines. This enables a refusal to consider Asians as serious candidates for leadership positions, producing a "bamboo ceiling" (Hyun, 2005) and the documented paucity of Asians and Asian Americans in leadership roles, even in STEM fields in which they have significant numeric representation (Lu et al., 2020). On the other hand, the unconsidered assumption that African American students are dangerous leads to criminalizing Black boys and girls through harsher and more frequent out-of-school discipline directly linking the segments of the school-to-prison pipeline (Welch et al., 2022). Complicating race-based discrimination is the history of linguistic discrimination, particularly against Latinx students (Scott & Venegas, 2017), not to mention the nearly complete erasure of indigenous groups (Sabzalian et al., 2021) through the "tender violence" of missionary boarding schools (Bauer, 2022). The resulting patterns of acting (Mezirow, 2000) have negative outcomes for non-White students which produce a vicious cycle with habits of mind, confirming them, making them seem natural, and apparently perpetuating continued patterns of acting in support of those habits of mind (Liu, 2020).

Many teacher education programs attempt to produce reflective teachers (Howard, 2003; Liu, 2011; Ross, 2014; Schon, 1983; Zeichner & Liston, 2013), but the pervasive mistreatment of minoritized students in the public schools described above strongly suggests that, far from encouraging anti-racist habits of mind and patterns of acting, the practices in teacher education programs fall short in transforming toxic habits of mind and patterns of acting. For example,

- Some teacher educators rarely talk about race or racism. Instead they focus their coursework and assignments on technical approaches toward teaching methods and classroom management (Carter Andrews et al., 2019; Ladson-Billings, 1996; Tatum, 2007).
- When teacher educators do discuss race or racism, they tend to tell prospective teachers what not to do in the classroom. They fail to engage with race and racism in a concrete fashion that would model anti-racist approaches for their prospective teachers (Chang-Bacon, 2022; Galman et al., 2010).
- Although teacher educators attempt to inculcate reflective practices—which are a vital element in anti-racist practice (Kishimoto, 2018)—among their prospective teachers, the use of reflective artifacts for assessment toward graduation and licensure encourages the presentation of a non-racial self immune to critical analysis (Liu, 2015, 2020; Thomas & Liu, 2012).
- Teacher educators often do not triangulate the statements prospective teachers make in their reflective writing by observing their actions in their placement classrooms (Cochran-Smith et al., 2015; Liu, 2011, 2015, 2020). This prevents teacher educators from seeing the racist patterns of acting prospective teachers bring into their classrooms.

Researchers have typically attempted to establish a picture of White prospective teachers' perceptions of race and racial attitudes through surveys (Howard, 2010), written reflections (Gay, 2010; Jackson et al., 2016) and, less frequently, interviews (Cooper, 2003). Much of this research has been situated in studies of specific courses in an effort to determine if such efforts do transform prospective teachers' habits of mind, and emphasizes "race-evasive" aspects of White teacher identity (Jupp et al., 2019). Earlier, one of the authors of this book, Liu (2020) did a thorough analysis of prospective teachers' written reflections in comparison to their classroom actions, going beyond prospective teachers' perceptions of teaching for social justice and equity. The findings demonstrated significant contradictions between the participants' articulations of teaching for social justice and equity and their real classroom practices, which included ignoring, segregating, and disciplining minoritized students. Building upon Liu's (2020) work, this book attempts to establish linkages between prospective teachers' habits of mind and patterns of acting regarding race and racism through a qualitative, longitudinal study of prospective teachers within three different teacher education programs; the goal was both to understand the social and institutional barriers to developing anti-racist teaching and teacher education, and to develop specific critically reflective teacher education practices that will enable generativity (Ball, 2009) and transformation toward anti-racist teaching and teacher education.

1.3   About This Book

Because our research questions focus on White prospective teachers' habits of mind and patterns of acting regarding race and racism in reflection and action, our theoretical framework comprises three elements: (1) Critical Race Theory (CRT); (2) Culturally relevant and sustaining community-based teacher education; and (3) critical reflection and generative change for transformative action. As described in Liu et al. (2023), we conceive of these three elements with the metaphor of a journey in which the destination is the "transformation of the educational system to effect educational equity" (p. 371). For this journey, CRT provides the roadmap to equity, while culturally relevant and sustaining community-based teacher education provides the vehicle to get there. The engine is powered by critical reflection and generative change for transformative action. Guided by this theoretical framework, we conducted a longitudinal qualitative study from 2008 to 2019 in three different elementary teacher education programs in three state universities situated in significantly different areas in the United States. Chapter 2 provides a detailed description of the theoretical framework and the research methodology. As we were going to press, the urgency of the challenges we face in fulfilling the mission outlined in this book intensified with the 2024 U.S. presidential elections. The campaigns and the aftermath are demonstrating very clearly that our society and institutions are starkly—and actively—riven by intergenerational racism and misogynoir. Preparing antiracist teachers is crucial to dismantle the patterns of thought and action that have proven to be so damaging to our students and our communities.

Preparing White Teachers for Antiracist Education is a study of persistent racism in thought and action among White prospective teachers, examining both how they conceive of race and racism ("habits of mind") and how they react when dealing with race and racism in the classroom (patterns of acting). With a firm grounding in real-world data, the book then details ways in which teacher educators can recognize and deal with prospective teachers who cannot—or will not—translate their reflections on race into actions against racism.

After the brief introduction in this chapter, we turn to Chap. 2, "Theoretical Framework and Research Design." This chapter begins with an explanation of the theoretical framework underpinning our work and this book, which employs counter-narrative in a process of critical reflection for generative transformation (Miller et al., 2020), all informed at every level by the insights of Critical Race Theory. The chapter then proceeds to describe the research context in which we developed the findings on habits of mind and patterns of acting discussed in Chaps. 3 and 4.

Chapter 3, "From Camouflage to Pledging Commitment," begins with a summary of Mezirow's notion of *habits of mind* and the ways in which it dovetails with related concepts from scholars of critical reflection, such as Brookfield and van Manen. We then explore the data from our research with White preservice teachers, identifying four common habits of mind found in written and spoken reflections. The first is *camouflaging*, the habit of speaking around race using terms such as "difference" or "diversity," or focusing on economic or social factors in lieu of racial issues. The second is *simplifying*, reducing race and racism to simple terms such as "culture" (left undefined) or constructing cross-race relationships solely in terms of personal affect, elided history, and power relations. The third is *holding deficit views toward minoritized students and criminalizing their behaviors*. The fourth common habit of mind is *pledging commitment*, the habit of responding to the statement of racial issues by articulating a promise to fight for equity at some unspecified point in the future. Pledging commitment, in its most extreme form, becomes a kind of soteriological stance we call *savior-making* in which White preservice teachers presented themselves as saving minority children from the negative consequences of their racial identity.

Chapter 4, "One Step Forward, Two Steps Back," briefly discusses Mezirow's notion of *patterns of acting*, explaining how patterns of acting link to habits of mind. We then go into the data from our research, identifying a key contradiction in White preservice teachers' classroom behavior between prepared performances of racial equity versus unexpected appearances of racial inequities. Specifically, through multiple teaching observations and interviews, we gained a deep understanding of their patterns of acting in the classroom. When there is an opportunity to carefully design a lesson, prospective teachers were able to perform some culturally relevant strategies. However, in unscripted situations, when interacting with students of color, they backslid, returning to a pattern of criminalizing and dehumanizing actions, and meting out capricious punishment. Even in the context of a prepared lesson, racism in the form of systemic subconscious institutional reinforcement can upend the plans, breaking through the planning to expose the race-based nature of the classroom experience.

Chapter 5, "Toward Anti-racist Teacher Education," returns to the theoretical basis for the book, CRT, to examine and challenge the habits of mind and patterns of acting reported in Chaps. 3 and 4, drawing out the larger social and institutional practices which shape White prospective teachers' approach to race. We then consider the implications for anti-racist teacher education programs, focusing specifically on the need to challenge White preservice teachers' unexamined assumptions about race and racism not just through readings and exercises in teacher education courses, but also through the entire field experience. We cannot emphasize too strongly the value of longitudinal engagement with anti-racist critical reflection, given the persistence of racist habits of mind and patterns of acting learned by growing up White in US society.

Chapter 6, "Cultivating Critical Reflection for Transformative Learning in the Context of Race," addresses ways in which we can restructure teacher education to develop anti-racist habits of mind and patterns of acting among White prospective teachers. We begin this chapter by revisiting the theoretical framework detailed in Chap. 2 with the argument that, although developed for research, this framework can guide teacher education program design and the preparation of White prospective teachers for anti-racist teaching. We then present a brief guide for developing and implementing community-based teacher education using the framework and insights of this book, using a series of reflective practice activities in coursework and classroom apprenticeship to cultivate habits of mind toward educational equity and patterns of acting to implement it.

Chapter 7, "The Potential to Achieve," proposes more radical changes to teacher education in the United States. Rather than thinking of the findings and suggestions of the previous chapters as palliative for a system that must be preserved, this chapter argues for a new generation of teacher education programs that centers transformative teacher education for educational equity in a holistic context of prospective teachers, university-based teacher educators, school-based mentor teachers, and the parents and community members the schools serve. We then present the experiences of two prospective teachers of color who were able to challenge dominant habits of mind regarding minoritized students of color and families and implement transformative actions to support them. Drawing from these authentic voices and experiences, we reimagine one of the key events recounted earlier in the book, constructing a counter-narrative to demonstrate how White preservice teachers can help in-service teachers, students, and communities transform racialized institutions and practices in service of educational justice and equity.

Finally, we offer here a note on the terminology regarding race and racism used in this book. Readers may or may not be aware of long-running debates over the use of specific labels signifying the positionality of various groups of people within racialized systems in the United States. For the purposes of this book, we capitalize the nouns identifying specific minoritized groups (Black, Latinx, Asian, Indigenous, Gay, and so forth). We also capitalized White and related ideologies and practices (such as Whiteness and White Supremacy) because White indicates a positioning with the racial system that must be acknowledged and dealt with; refusing to capitalize White as a racialized category is "an anti-Black act which frames Whiteness as both neutral and the standard" (Nguyễn & Pendleton, 2020). When we wish to refer to a range of groups with differing relations to Whiteness as well as to each other within the racialized systems of the United States, we use the phrase "minoritized groups" in order to emphasize "the connection of status to power differentials" and the taking of power from certain groups (American Medical Association, 2021, p. 13). When similar terms appear in quoted material, however, whether that be academic writings or the words of our research participants, we use the terms they use without modification.

References

American Medical Association and Association of American Medical Colleges. (2021). *Advancing health equity: Guide on language, narrative and concepts.* https://www.ama-assn.org/equity-guide

Andrews, D. J. C., Brown, T., Castillo, B. M., Jackson, D., & Vellanki, V. (2019). Beyond damage-centered teacher education: Humanizing pedagogy for teacher educators and preservice teachers. *Teachers College Record, 121*(6), 1–28.

Annamma, S. A., Anyon, Y., Joseph, N. M., Farrar, J., Greer, E., Downing, B., & Simmons, J. (2019). Black girls and school discipline: The complexities of being overrepresented and understudied. *Urban Education, 54*(2), 211–242.

Au, K., & Jordan, C. (1981). Teaching reading to Hawaiian children: Finding a *culturally appropriate solution.* In H. T. Trueba, G. P. Guthrie, & K. Au (Eds.), *Culture and the bilingual classroom: Studies in classroom ethnography* (pp. 139–152).

Balfanz, R., Byrnes, V., & Fox, J. H. (2015). Sent home and put off track: The antecedents, disproportionalities, and consequences of being suspended in the 9th grade. In D. J. Lose (Ed.), *Closing the school discipline gap: Equitable remedies for excessive exclusion* (pp. 17–30). Teachers College Press.

Ball, A. F. (2009). Toward a theory of generative change in culturally and linguistically complex classrooms. *American Educational Research Journal, 46*(1), 45–72.

Ball, D. L., & Forzani, F. M. (2009). The work of teaching and the challenge for teacher education. *Journal of Teacher Education, 60*(5), 497–511.

Banks, J. A. (2006). *Cultural diversity and education: Foundations, curriculum, and teaching.* 5th illustrated ed. Pearson.

Banks, J. A. (2013). The construction and historical development of multicultural education, 1962–2012. *Theory into Practice, 52*(1), 73–82.

Banks, J. A., & Banks, C. A. M. (1995). *Handbook of research on multicultural education.* Macmillan.

Basile, V., York, A., & Black, R. (2019). Who is the one being disrespectful? Understanding and deconstructing the criminalization of elementary school boys of color. *Urban Education, 57*(9), 1592–1620.

Bauer, N. K. (2022). *Tender violence in U.S. schools: Benevolent Whiteness and the dangers of heroic white womanhood.* Routledge.

Blaisdell, B. (2016). Schools as racial spaces: Understanding and resisting structural racism. *International Journal of Qualitative Studies in Education, 29*(2), 248–272.

Bonilla, Y., & Rosa, J. (2015). #Ferguson: Digital protest, hashtag ethnography, and the racial politics of social media in the United States. *American Ethnologist, 42*(2), 4–17.

Bonilla-Silva, E. (2001). *White supremacy and racism in the post-civil rights era.* Lynne Rienner Publishers.

Bonilla-Silva, E. (2012). The invisible weight of whiteness: The racial grammar of everyday life in America. *Michigan Sociological Review, 26*(Fall), 1–15.

Brown, K., Skiba, R. J., & Eckes Suzanne, E. (2009). African American disproportionality in school discipline: The divide between best evidence and legal remedy. *The New York Law School Law Review, 54*, 1071.

Brown, K. D. (2014). Teaching in color: A critical race theory in education analysis of the literature on preservice teachers of color and teacher education in the US. *Race Ethnicity and Education, 17*(3), 326–345.

Bryan, N. (2017). White teachers; role in sustaining the school-to-prison pipeline: Recommendations for teacher education. *The Urban Review, 49*, 326–345.

Capella-Santana, N. (2003). Voices of teacher candidates: Positive changes in multicultural attitudes and knowledge. *The Journal of Educational Research, 96*(3), 182–190.

Carter Andrews, D. J. (2009). "The hardest thing to turn from:" The effects of service learning on preparing urban educators. *Equity & Excellence in Education, 42*(3), 272–293.

Case, K. A., & Hemmings, A. (2005). Distancing strategies: White women preservice teachers and antiracist curriculum. *Urban Education, 40*(6), 606–662.

Chan, S. (1996). The writing of Asian American history. *OAH Magazine of History, 10*(4), 8–17.

Chang-Bacon, C. K. (2022). "We Sort of Dance Around the Race Thing:" Race-evasiveness in teacher education. *Journal of Teacher Education, 73*(1), 8–22.

Cochran-Smith, M., Villegas, A. M., Abrams, L., Chavez-Moreno, L., Mills, T., & Stern, R. (2015). Critiquing teacher preparation research: An overview of the field II. *Journal of Teacher Education, 56*(2), 109–121.

Cooper, P. M. (2003). Effective White teachers of Black children: Teaching within a community. *Journal of Teacher Education, 54*(5), 413–427.

Dedeoglu, H., & Lamme, L. L. (2011). Selected demographics, attitudes, and beliefs about diversity of preservice teachers. *Education and Urban Society, 43*(4), 468–485.

Dee, J. R., & Henkin, A. B. (2002). Assessing dispositions toward cultural diversity among preservice teachers. *Urban Education, 37*(1), 22–40.

Deloria, V., Jr. (1969). *Custer died for your sins: An Indian manifesto.* Macmillan.

Delpit, L. (2006). *Other people's children: Cultural conflict in the classroom.* First Revised ed., First Published 1995. New Press.

DuBois, W. E. B. (1903). *The souls of Black folk.* A.C. McClurg & Co.

Ducey, E. M., Jr. (2013). *White teachers, Latino students: A case study of the extent of cultural responsiveness learned in a teacher education program.* Unpublished Ed.D. dissertation. University of Memphis.

Fadus, M. C., Ginsburg, K. R., Sobowale, K., Halliday-Boykins, C. A., Bryant, B. E., Gray, K. M., & Squeglia, L. M. (2020). Unconscious bias and the diagnosis of disruptive behavior disorders and ADHD in African American and Hispanic youth. *Academic Psychiatry, 44,* 95–102.

Feistritzer, C. E. (2011). *Profile of teachers in the U.S.: 2011.* National Center for Education Information.

Gainer, J. S., & Larrotta, C. (2010). Reproducing and interrupting subtractive schooling in teacher education. *Multicultural Education, 17*(3), 41–47.

Galman, S., Pica-Smith, C., & Rosenberger, C. (2010). Aggressive and tender navigations: Teacher educators confront whiteness in their practice. *Journal of Teacher Education, 61*(3), 225–236.

Gao, S., Liu, K., & McKinney, M. (2019). Learning formative assessment in the field: Analysis of reflective conversations between preservice teachers and their classroom mentors. *International Journal of Mentoring and Coaching in Education, 8*(3), 197–216.

Gay, G. (2000). *Culturally responsive teaching: Theory, research, and practice: 2nd edition.* Multicultural education series. Teachers College Press.

Gay, G. (2010). Acting on beliefs in education for cultural diversity. *Journal of Teacher Education, 6*(1–2), 143–152.

Goff, P. A., Jackson, M. C., Di Leone, B. A. L., Culotta, C. M., & DiTomasso, N. A. (2014). The essence of innocence: Consequences of dehumanizing Black children. *Journal of Personality and Social Psychology, 104*(6), 526–545.

Grant, C. A., & Sleeter, C. E. (2007). *Doing multicultural education for achievement and equity.* Routledge.

Hambacher, E. (2017). Resisting punitive school discipline: Perspectives and practices of exemplary urban elementary teachers. *International Journal of Qualitative Studies in Education, 31*(2), 102–118.

Howard, T. C. (2003). Culturally relevant pedagogy: Ingredients for critical teacher reflection. *Theory into Practice, 42*(3), 195–202.

Howard, T. C. (2010). *Why race and culture matter in schools: Closing the achievement gap in America's classrooms.* Teachers College Press.

Hyun, J. (2005). *Breaking the bamboo ceiling: Career strategies for Asians.* Harper Business.

Ingersoll, R., May, H., & Collins, G. (2017). *Minority teacher recruitment, employment and retention: 1987 to 2013.* LPI Research Report. Learning Policy Institute, Palo Alto.

Jackson, T. O., Bryan, M. L., & Larkin, M. L. (2016). An analysis of White pre-service teachers' reflections on race and young children within an urban school context. *Urban Education, 51*(1), 60–81.

Johnson, T. (2020). "When Black people are in pain, White people just join book clubs." *The Washington Post,* June 11, 2020.

Jupp, J. C., Leckie, A., Cabrera, N. L., & Utt, J. (2019). Race-evasive white teacher identity studies 1990–2015: What can we learn from 25 years of research? *Teachers College Record, 121*(1), 1–58.

Kishimoto, K. (2018). Anti-racist pedagogy: From faculty's self-reflection to orga-nizing within and beyond the classroom. *Race Ethnicity and Education, 21*(4), 540–554.

Kohlii, R. (2008). Breaking the cycle of racism in the classroom: Critical race reflections from future teachers of color. *Teacher Education Quarterly, 35*(4), 177–188.

Kohlii, R., Pizarro, M., & Nevárez, A. (2017). The "new racism" of K-12 schools: Centering critical research on racism. *Review of Research in Education, 41*(1), 182–202.

Ladson-Billings, G. (1995). Toward a theory of culturally relevant pedagogy. *American Educational Research Journal, 32*(3), 465–491.

Ladson-Billings, G. (1996). Silences as weapons: Challenges of a Black professor teaching White students. *Theory into Practice, 35*(2), 79–85.

Ladson-Billings, G. (1999). Preparing teachers for diverse student populations: A critical race theory perspective. *Review of Research in Education, 24*(1), 211–247.

Ladson-Billings, G. (2000). Fighting for our lives: Preparing teachers to teach African American students. *Journal of Teacher Education, 51*(3), 206–214.

Ladson-Billings, G. (2006). From the achievement gap to the education debt: Understanding achievement in U.S. public schools. *Educational Researcher, 35*(7), 3–12.

Ladson-Billings, G. (2014). Culturally relevant pedagogy 2.0: The remix. *Harvard Educational Review, 84*(1), 74–84.

Ladson-Billings, G. (2021). Three decades of culturally relevant, responsive, and sustaining pedagogy: What lies ahead? *The Educational Forum, 85*(4), 351–354.

Ladson-Billings, G., & Ball, A. F. (2020). Educating teachers for the 21st century: Culture, reflection, and learning. In N. S. Nasir, C. D. Lee, R. Pea, & M. McKinney de Royston (Eds.), *Handbook of the cultural foundations of learn-ing* (pp. 387–403). Routledge.

Ladson-Billings, G., & Donnor, J. (2008). The moral activist role of critical race theory scholarship. In N. K. Denzin, Y. S. Lincoln, & L. T. Smith (Eds.), *Handbook of critical and indigenous methodologies* (pp. 279–301). Sage.

Liu, K. (2011). Enhancing prospective teachers' critical reflection in the ePortfolio environment. Ph.D. dissertation, University of Wisconsin-Madison.

Liu, K. (2015). Critical reflection as a framework for transformative learning in teacher education. *Educational Review, 67*(2), 135–157.

Liu, K. (2020). *Critical reflection for transformative learning.* Springer.

Liu, K., & Ball, A. F. (2019). Critical reflection and generativity: Toward a framework of transformative teacher education for diverse learners. *Review of Research in Education, 43*(1), 68–105.

Liu, K., Miller, R., & Ball, A. F. (2023). Teacher education for diverse learners. In R. J. Tierney, F. Rizvi, & K. Erkican (Eds.), *International Encyclopedia of education, vol. 5* (pp. 356–367). Elsevier.

Lortie, D. C. (1975). *Schoolteacher: A sociological study.* University of Chicago Press.

Losen, D. J., Hodson, C. L., Keith, M. A., II, Morrison, K., & Belway, S. (2015). *Are we closing the school discipline gap?* UCLA Center for Civil Rights Remedies. https://escholarship.org/content/qt2t36g571/qt2t36g571.pdf

Lu, J., Nisbett, R. E., & Morris, M. W. (2020). Why East Asians but not South Asians are underrepresented in leadership positions in the United States. *Proceedings of the National Academy of Sciences, 117*(9), 4590–4600.

Marchbanks, M. P., III, Blake, J. J., Booth, E. A., Carmichael, D., Seibert, A. L., & Fabelo, T. (2015). The economic effects of exclusionary discipline on grade retention and high school dropout. In D. J. Lowen (Ed.), *Closing the school discipline gap: Equitable remedies for excessive exclusion* (pp. 59–74). Teachers College Press.

Matias, C. E., & Zembylas, M. (2014). "When saying you care is not really caring:" Emotions of disgust, whiteness ideology, and teacher education. *Critical Studies in Education, 55*(3), 319–337.

McIntyre, A. (1997). *Making meaning of whiteness: Exploring racial identity with white teachers.* State University of New York Press.

Mezirow, J. (Ed.). (1990). *Fostering critical reflection in adulthood: A guide to transformative and emancipatory learning.* Jossey-Bass.

Mezirow, J. (1997). Transformative learning: Theory to practice. *New Directions for Adult and Continuing Education, 1997*(74), 5–12.

Mezirow, J. (2000). *Learning as transformation: Critical perspectives on a theory in progress.* Jossey-Bass.

Mezirow, J. (2003). How critical reflection triggers transformative learning. *Adult and Continuing Education: Teaching, Learning and Research, 4*, 199–213.

Miller, R., Liu, K., & Ball, A. F. (2020). Critical counter-narrative as transformative methodology for educational equity. *Review of Research in Education, 44*(1), 269–300.

Milner, H. R. (2010). *Start where you are, but don't stay there: Understanding diversity, opportunity gaps, and teaching in today's Classrooms.* Harvard Education Press.

Milner, H. R. (2012). But What is urban education? *Urban Education, 47*(3), 556–561. https://doi.org/10.1177/0042085912447516

Milner, H. R. (2023). *The race card: Leading the fight for truth in America's schools.* Corwin Press.

Mohatt, G., & Erickson, F. (1981). Cultural differences in teaching styles in an Odawa school: A sociolinguistic approach. In H. T. Trueba, G. P. Guthrie, & K. H. Au (Eds.), *Culture and the bilingual classroom* (pp. 105–138). Newbury House Publishers.

Moll, L. C., Amanti, C., Neff, D., & Gonzalez, N. (1992). Funds of knowledge for teaching: Using a qualitative approach to connect homes and classrooms. *Theory into Practice, 31*(2), 132–141.

Morris, E. W., & Perry, B. L. (2016). The punishment gap: School suspension and racial disparities in achievement. *Social Problems, 63*(1), 68–86.

National Center for Education Statistics. (2023). Characteristics of Public School Teachers. *Condition of Education.* U.S. Department of Education, Institute of Education Sciences. Retrieved June 5, 2024, from https://nces.ed.gov/programs/coe/indicator/clr

National Center for Education Statistics. (2024). Racial/Ethnic Enrollment in Public Schools. *Condition of Education.* U.S. Department of Education, Institute of Education Sciences. Retrieved June 1, 2024, from https://nces.ed.gov/programs/coe/indicator/cge

Nguyễn, A. T., & Pendleton, M. (2020). Recognizing race in language: Why we capitalize "Black" and "White." Center for the Study of Social Policy Ideas Into Action, March 23. https://cssp.org/2020/03/recognizing-race-in-language-why-we-capitalize-black-and-white

Owens, J., & McLanahan, S. S. (2020). Unpacking the drivers of racial disparities in school suspension and expulsion. *Social Forces, 98*(4), 1548–1577.

Paine, L. (1990). *Orientation towards diversity: What do prospective teachers bring?* Michigan State University National Center for Research on Teacher Education. Retrieved from https://eric.ed.gov/?id=ED320903

Pane, D. M., & Rocco, T. S. (2014). *Transforming the school-to-prison pipeline: Lessons from the classroom.* Educational futures: Rethinking theory and practice. Sense Publishers.

Paris, D. (2012). Culturally sustaining pedagogy: A needed change in stance, terminology, and practice. *Educational Researcher, 41*(3), 93–97.

Paris, D., & Alim, H. S. (2017). *Culturally sustaining pedagogies: Teaching and learning for justice in a changing world.* Language and literacy series. Teachers College Press.

Paris, D., & Ball, A. F. (2009). Teacher knowledge in culturally and linguistically complex classrooms: Lessons from the golden age and beyond. In L. M. Morrow, R. Rueda, & D. Lapp (Eds.), *Handbook of research on literacy instruction: Issues of diversity, policy, and equity* (pp. 379–395). Guilford.

Picower, B., & Kohli, R. (Eds.). (2017). *Confronting racism in teacher education: Counternarratives of critical practice.* Taylor & Francis.

Pollock, M., Deckman, S., Mira, M., & Shalaby, C. (2010). "But what can I do?": Three necessary tensions in teaching teachers about race. *Journal of Teacher Education, 61*(3), 211–224.

Ray, R. (2022). School as a Hostile Institution: How black and immigrant girls of color experience the classroom. *Gender & Society, 36*(1), 88–111.

Richardson, V. (1996). The role of attitudes and beliefs in learning to teach. *Handbook of Research on Teacher Education, 2*(102–119), 273–290.

Ross, J. (2014). Engaging with "webness" in online reflective writing practices. *Computers and Composition, 34*, 96–109.

Sabzalian, L., Shear, S. B., & Snyder, J. (2021). Standardizing Indigenous erasure: A TribalCrit and QuantCrit analysis of K-12 US civics and government standards. *Theory & Research in Social Education, 47*(3), 321–359.

Schon, D. A. (1983). *The reflective practitioner.* Basic Books.

Scott, L. M., & Venegas, E. M. (2017). Linguistic hegemony today: Recommendations for eradicating language discrimination. *Journal for Multicultural Education, 11*(1), 19–30.

Seattlage, J. (2011). Counterstories from White mainstream preservice teachers: Resisting the master narrative of deficit by default. *Cultural Studies of Science Education, 6*, 803–836.

Skiba, R. J., Horner, R. H., Chung, C., Rausch, M. K., May, S., & Tobin, T. (2011). Race is not neutral: A national investigation of African American and Latino disproportionality in school discipline. *School Psychology Review, 40*, 85–107.

Sleeter, C. E. (2001). Preparing teachers for culturally diverse schools: Research and the overwhelming presence of whiteness. *Journal of Teacher Education, 52*(2), 94–106.

Sleeter, C. E. (2008). Preparing white teachers for diverse students. In M. Cochran-Smith, S. Feiman-Nemser, & D. J. McIntyre (Eds.), *Handbook of research on teacher education: Enduring questions in changing contexts* (pp. 559–582). Routledge.

Sleeter, C. E. (2017). Critical race theory and the whiteness of teacher education. *Urban Education, 52*(2), 155–169.

Sleeter, C. E., Neal, L. I., & Kumashiro, K. K. (2015). *Diversifying the teacher workforce: Preparing and retaining highly effective teachers.* Routledge.

Takaki, R. (1998). *Strangers from a distant shore: A history of Asian Americans.* Little, Brown & Company.

Tatum, B. D. (2007). *Can we talk about race? And other conversations in an era of school resegregation.* Beacon Press.

Thomas, M. K., & Liu, K. (2012). The performance of reflection: A grounded analysis of prospective teachers' ePortfolios. *Journal of Technology and Teacher Education, 20*(3), 305–330.

U.S. Department of Education Office of Civil Rights. (2023). *2020–21 Civil rights data collection: Student discipline and school climate in U.S. public schools*. New data release November 2023. https://www2.ed.gov/about/offices/list/ocr/docs/crdc-2020-21.html

Utt, J., & Tochluk, S. (2020). White teacher, know thyself: Improving anti-racist praxis through racial identity development. *Urban Education, 55*(1), 125–152.

Valencia, R. R. (2010). *Dismantling contemporary deficit thinking: Educational thought and practice*. Routledge.

Valli, L. (1995). The dilemma of race: Learning to be color blind and color conscious. *Journal of Teacher Education, 46*(2), 120–129.

Villegas, A. M., & Irvine, J. J. (2010). Diversifying the teaching force: An examination of major arguments. *The Urban Review, 42*, 175–192.

Walker-Dalhouse, D., & Dalhouse, A. D. (2006). Investigating White preservice teachers' beliefs about teaching in culturally diverse classrooms. *Negro Educational Review, 57*(1/2), 69–84, 140–141.

Welch, K., Lehmann, P. S., Chouhy, C., & Chiricos, T. (2022). Cumulative racial and ethnic disparities along the school-to-prison pipeline. *Journal of Research in Crime and Delinquency, 59*(5), 574–626.

Wiley, K. E. (2021). A tale of two logics: School discipline and racial disparities in a "mostly white" middle school. *American Journal of Education, 127*(2), 163–192.

Woodson, C. G. (1933). *The mis-education of the Negro*. Associated Publishers.

Wun, C. (2014). Unaccounted foundations: Black girls, anti-black racism, and punishment in schools. *Critical Sociology, 42*(4–5), 737–750.

Zeichner, K., & Liston, D. (2013). *Reflective teaching: An introduction* (2nd ed.). Routledge.

Zeichner, K., Payne, K. A., & Brayko, K. (2016). Democratizing teacher education. *Journal of Teacher Education, 66*(2), 122–135.

Zimmermann, C. R. (2018). The penalty of being a young Black girl: Kindergarten teachers' perceptions of children's problem behaviors and student-teacher conflict by the intersection of race and gender. *Journal of Negro Education, 87*(2), 154–168.

CHAPTER 2

Theoretical Framework and Research Design: Seeing Through the Prism of Anti-racism

As discussed in Chap. 1, the US public school teaching force has remained majority White even as the student population has become majority minority. Given this reality, teacher education programs have taken multiple approaches to prepare White prospective teachers to teach diverse student populations. These approaches include multicultural education (Banks, 1974, 1995; Banks & Banks, 2010; Bullivant, 1972; Gay, 1977; Grant, 1975; Grant & Koskela, 1986), culturally relevant pedagogy (Ladson-Billings, 1995; Ladson-Billings, 2014; Ladson-Billings, 2021), culturally responsive teaching (Gay, 2000, 2002), culturally sustaining pedagogy (Paris, 2012; Paris & Alim, 2017), and explicitly anti-racist pedagogy (Howard, 2016; Kishimoto, 2018; Kumashiro, 2003; Ladson-Billings, 1999; Love, 2019, 2023; Milner, 2007, 2015, 2021, 2023). If we consider collectively these approaches to preparing teachers for minoritized students—working to improve the disposition and practice of White teachers—there appear to be great accomplishments in theory but significant shortfalls in practice. Multiple studies (DePalma, 2010; Evans-Winters & Hoff, 2011; Gist, 2017; Han, 2014; Horton & Scott, 2004; Matias & Mackey, 2016) indicate that the habits of privilege on the part of White prospective teachers and the pervasive Whiteness of structures and practices in teacher education programs amplify the voices of White prospective teachers and teacher educators and silence those of prospective teachers and faculty of color. As a result, many teacher education

K. Liu et al., *Preparing White Teachers for Anti-Racist Education*, https://doi.org/10.1007/978-3-031-73534-9_2

programs continue to produce White teachers who are at best ineffective in working with diverse student populations. After decades of research and writing on educational inequality, how did this dismal situation come about?

2.1   ADDRESSING THE ROOTS OF INEQUITY THROUGH TRANSFORMATIVE PRAXIS

A review of the literature on preparing teachers for minoritized students indicates three fundamental problems, all stemming from a loss of emphasis on the deep roots of inequality and inequity in schooling, and a concomitant lack of focus on transformative action by teachers. First is the fundamental problem of Whiteness in teaching and teacher education (Picower, 2009). White prospective teachers need support to fully analyze racialized teacher education programs and critique the dominant social order. If teacher educators wish to teach prospective teachers to implement culturally relevant and sustaining pedagogies and anti-racist teaching in their future practice, they should implement these pedagogies throughout the programs, building curriculum and field experience on the lived experiences of the minoritized student populations and the cultural capital from their communities (Yosso, 2005). Changing habits of mind takes time and therefore the common, one-shot solution of introducing these pedagogies as an add-on to an existing White curriculum and practice does not lead to White prospective teachers' transformative learning. Although teacher education programs have made efforts to recruit and prepare more teachers of color (Liu, et al., 2017; Valenzuela, 2017, Villegas & Irvine, 2010; Villegas et al., 2012; Woodson & Pabon, 2016), the Whiteness in teacher education programs fails their learning needs (Sleeter, 2017). Once students of color become teacher education candidates, their programs are often predominantly White (Ladson-Billings, 1995), with curriculum, pedagogy, methods, and field experiences constructed to center Whiteness as the norm, and thus fail to provide the types of social, cultural, emotional, and academic support that students of color need to successfully complete their programs (Bryan, 2021; Gist, 2014, 2017; Kohli, 2019; Sleeter & Thao, 2007). Prospective teachers of color then encounter marginalization and discrimination in teacher education courses and field placement schools similar to their experiences in the K-12 system (Burant, 1999; Gay, 2005; Irizarry, 2007; Liu, 2020; Parker & Hood, 1995; Rodriguez-Mojica et al., 2020; Sleeter, 2001; Villegas & Davis,

2008). Second is the problem of interest convergence. Although research shows that exposure to minoritized students and communities improves the ability of White prospective teachers to empathize with students of color and increase their awareness of racism (Milner, 2006), scholars have also repeatedly observed that race rarely has a central place in American teacher education (Milner, 2003, 2017; Milner & Laughter, 2015). Moreover, the "empathic fallacy" (Delgado & Stefancic, 2017)—the idea that becoming aware of the humanity of minoritized students and their communities will automatically produce anti-racist teaching on the part of White teachers—is clearly belied by the persistence of deficit thinking and discriminatory practices in US schools and schooling. It appears, then, that learning about minoritized students and communities occurs, but only to the extent that it enriches White teachers and students, not to the point that it effects real change in the perception and treatment of minoritized students. Brown (2014) critiqued these efforts, stating that

> While the call for recruiting more teachers of color is well founded, they exist in and help to maintain a system of interest convergence wherein teacher education programs can boast about efforts to bring in more teacher candidates of color while simultaneously not transforming the kinds of normative culture, knowledge, and experiences that are valued, maintained, and offered to these individuals. (pp. 339–340)

The third fundamental problem is the lack of attention to practice—how or whether preservice teachers implement anti-racist teaching to support minoritized learners in their classrooms (Anderson & Stillman, 2013; Cochran-Smith et al., 2015; Liu, 2015, 2020). By practice, we mean "teacher candidates learning how to do the actual tasks of teaching" (Cochran-Smith et al., 2015, p. 117). However, much research that intends to study how teacher preparation influences prospective teachers' professional practice does not investigate their actions in classroom contexts because practice is considered to be "teacher candidates being engaged as reflective and inquiring professionals" (Cochran-Smith et al., 2015, p. 117). This type of research has primarily engaged prospective teachers in talking about, analyzing, or reflecting on their teaching, and thus research data on practice is primarily based on prospective teachers' reflections, self-reports, surveys, and interviews, but has not made an effort to ground-truth those reflective artifacts with classroom observations.

Based on a thorough review of research on the preparation of teachers for urban and high-needs schools, Anderson and Stillman (2013) found a disproportionate emphasis on belief and attitude change among prospective teachers with relatively little evidence for the development or change in actual teaching practice. They also found a tendency toward reductive views of culture and context. Cochran-Smith et al. (2015) argued that "we need more research that goes beyond assuming that changing teacher candidates' beliefs necessarily leads to different behaviors and actions in their classrooms" (p. 117). Research grounded in observations of classroom teaching indicates that in spite of required training on multicultural education and teaching for social justice, most White preservice and in-service teachers do not actually internalize these approaches or the philosophy underlying them. Rather, they are adept at performing a shallow approximation when given incentives and the opportunity to construct a carefully bounded example—but otherwise operate actively to protect and maintain Whiteness within the unconsidered privilege structure of the White majority (Conrad et al., 2023; Gao et al., 2019; Liu, 2011, 2020). We argue that teacher educators need to move beyond research on prospective teachers' attitudes and perspectives about teaching minoritized students to rigorous explorations of how they teach, what they teach, and how their teaching impacts the learning and life of minoritized learners based on their day-to-day practices. We further argue that this type of classroom practice-based research is time-consuming and needs to deliberately take time into consideration in research and teacher education curriculum design in order to see prospective teachers' growth and transformation. It is vital that the life and learning of minoritized learners be taken seriously and be used as first-hand data for teacher educators to transform their curriculum, pedagogy, and instruction.

2.2   TRANSFORMATIVE TEACHER EDUCATION FOR ANTI-RACIST TEACHING: A THEORETICAL FRAMEWORK

Because our research questions focus on White prospective teachers' habits of mind and patterns of acting regarding race and racism in reflection and teaching, we suggest a comprehensive reimagination of teacher education starting from the theoretical orientation through the institutional structures and practices down to the preparation of the individual prospective teacher. We envision this reimagination as a set of nested practices,

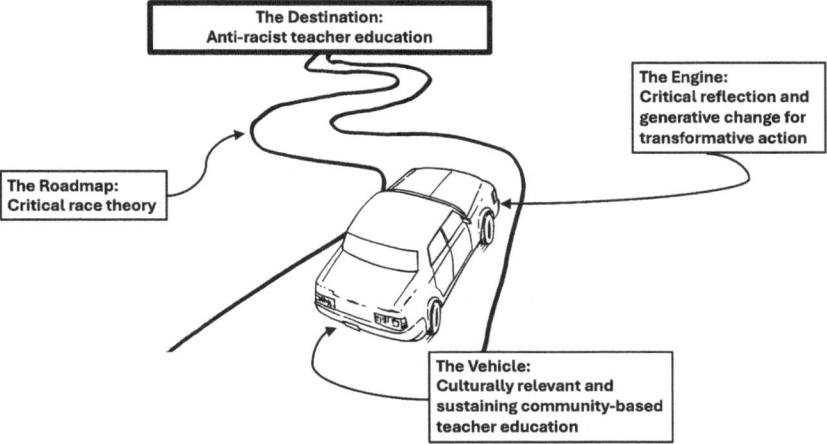

Fig. 2.1 Transformative teacher education for anti-racist teaching

each of which performs a different function while supporting the functioning of the other practices, much like physical travel requires a roadmap, a vehicle, and an engine (Fig. 2.1). Here, however, the destination is not a physical one but a social and political one: transformation of the educational system to center anti-racist education. Our theoretical framework comprises three elements: (1) Critical Race Theory (CRT); (2) Culturally relevant and sustaining community-based teacher education; and (3) critical reflection and generative change for transformative action. As described in Liu et al. (2023), we conceive of these three elements with the metaphor of travel in which the destination is the transformation of the educational system and practices to enhance educational equity. For this journey, CRT provides the roadmap to equity, culturally relevant and sustaining community-based teacher education provides the vehicle to get there, and the engine is powered by critical reflection and generative change for transformative action (Fig. 2.1).

2.3 THE DESTINATION: ANTI-RACIST EDUCATION

Being racist is, for most people, a negative thing, a feature of a person's worldview that should be eliminated. Indeed, many teachers, perhaps even most, proclaim themselves "not a racist;" some teacher education programs require such proclamations to graduate or even to be admitted.

Increasingly, however, teacher educators have come to the understanding that extracting proclamations of not-being-a-racist has not been an effective approach to producing teachers able to dismantle racism in our classroom, our schools, and our communities (Earick, 2009; Jupp et al., 2019; Kohli & Pizarro, 2022; Liu, 2020). The chapters that follow document many of the ways that teacher education programs have failed to go beyond proclamations of not-being-a-racist; these boil down to (1) a conception of racism that overemphasizes personal prejudice and sidesteps social privilege and institutional practices, and (2) teacher training that relies on the performance of not-being-a-racist to assess preservice teachers' attitudes toward minoritized students. In this book we advocate a different approach, *anti-racism*. Anti-racist teacher education, understood broadly as producing teachers able and willing to actively remedy and repair racist systems and practices, requires significant transformation in teacher education curriculum and pedagogy, some examples of which we detail later in this book. Here we briefly sketch out the rise of anti-racism in teacher education, and how anti-racism as a destination functions in our model for teacher education.

Anti-racism as a general practice in the United States, as Herbert Aptheker observed in his groundbreaking essay "Some Introductory Remarks: The History of Anti-Racism in the United States" (1975), is probably as old as racism itself. Moreover, continued Aptheker,

> Du Bois once remarked that the history of the United States in large part consisted of the position and treatment of black people and the response thereto; in similar vein one may affirm that racism and the struggle against it constitute a significant component of and, in many ways, a basic axis around which revolves much of the history of the United States. (p. 18)

At the time Aptheker wrote those words, far more attention had been paid inside and outside academia to racism, but comparatively little to anti-racism; it would be nearly another twenty years before Aptheker completed the first book-length history of antiracism in US history (Aptheker, 1992). Yet Oamek (2023) found that success in a teacher education program that attempted to incorporate anti-racist principles hinged on preservice teachers' access to learning and identity resources supporting their development, resources that are still scarce.

Anti-racism as an explicitly named approach in education emerges from CRT and multicultural education in the late 1970s and early 1980s across the English-speaking world (Finn, 1985; Lee, 1985; Washington, 1981, Watson, 1988). As in these related pedagogical discourses, anti-racism includes an effort to identify and uproot personally held prejudices, and also to make efforts to address racism outside oneself. Blum (1992) summed it up by saying,

> Antiracism [he also called it "opposition to racism"] as a value involves striving to be without racist attitudes oneself as well as being prepared to work against both racist attitudes in others and racial injustice in society more generally. (p. 2)

Blum's approach to race in general has been heavily criticized as leaning too strongly toward deliberate racial antipathy, and therefore providing a defense of "innocence" for White privilege and race-evasiveness (see, for example, Sundstrom, 2003). Nevertheless, his definition does encapsulate an important aspect of anti-racism: It is both inward-looking (striving to be without racist attitudes) and outward-acting (working against both racist attitudes in others and racial injustice in society). Most approaches to anti-racism aim to promote equity, inclusion, and social justice by challenging systems of oppression and empowering students to become critical thinkers and agents of change (Berman & McLaughlin, 1975; Mansfield & Kehoe, 1994) by acknowledging and confronting privilege, centering marginalized voices and perspectives, fostering critical consciousness, and advocating for systemic change in the direction of social justice and equity (hooks, 1994). Anti-racist educators engage in critical reflection and action, examine their own biases, and actively work to create learning environments that are anti-oppressive and affirming for all students (Arneback, 2022). Moreover, many approaches to anti-racist education are explicitly intersectional, dealing with "race and the intersection of social differences (class, gender, sexuality, race, and ethnicity)" (Dei & James, 1999, p. 96).

The historical development of anti-racism in education has not occurred without criticism, however. One early concern is lack of specificity in definition and implementation of policy. For example, the 1985 UK Ministry of Education report *Education for All* (Swann Report, 1985) called for multicultural/anti-racist education; three years later Watson (1988) summarized criticism of the results in terms of "incoherence," noting that the Swann Report called for "permeating every subject on the curriculum with a multicultural dimension," but then failed to indicate what exactly "permeate" meant, what exactly a "subject" might be, or how this permeation might be accomplished (p. 546). On the other hand, Ellsworth (1989), in dissecting her own education course on race and the media, developed a deeper pedagogical and philosophical critique, arguing that anti-racist pedagogy needed to be careful not to replace racist orthodoxy with another, albeit critical, orthodoxy and thereby guiding student voices and agency into predetermined channels. Finally, the article by Tre Johnson (*The Washington Post*, June 11, 2020) with which we began Chap. 1, "When Black people are in pain, White people just join book clubs," points to the problems that can arise when anti-racist teaching and teacher education focuses so closely on the desire of White participants to understand and empathize—the inward-looking element of anti-racism— that the outward-looking elements of advocacy and action are left undone.

In our model of anti-racist teacher education, we employ anti-racism in both its inward and outward aspects as the destination, the goal for both teachers and teacher educators. In Chaps. 5 and 6 we explain in some detail how we attempt to move toward that goal in terms of expectations and procedures in our teacher education programs. In the remainder of this chapter, we explain the model informing those expectations and procedures.

2.4   The Roadmap for Transformation: Critical Race Theory

Critical Race Theory (CRT) as a theoretical framework and set of related practices emerged from the field of legal studies and has since been applied to various disciplines, including education, sociology, political science, and more. It originated in the United States in the late 1970s and 1980s as a response to traditional approaches to civil rights and race relations. While often misunderstood or oversimplified, there are some key tenets or hypotheses that are advanced with CRT. The first is that race should be thought of as a *Social Construct*. CRT challenges the idea that race is a natural, biological category, emphasizing instead that it is a socially constructed concept with significant implications for power dynamics and social structures. CRT also recognizes that race intersects with other social categories like gender, class, sexuality, and coloniality, and emphasizes the importance of considering these intersecting identities when analyzing issues of inequity and discrimination. Also important is the idea of *Interest Convergence*. This concept suggests that progress toward racial equality is more likely to occur when the interests of marginalized racial groups align with the interests of those in power. In other words, positive changes are more likely when they benefit the dominant group as well as the minoritized group. CRT also emphasizes the existence of structural and systemic forms of racism embedded in laws, policies, and institutions. In this way, CRT does not view racism as simply something that exists in interpersonal relationships or within individual psyches. Rather, CRT critiques the idea that racism is only about individual prejudice, arguing that broader societal structures contribute to racial disparities. Racism is thus not understood as a rare aberration in fundamentally egalitarian social and political systems, but as ubiquitous, systemic, and "normal" within systems built with racism from the ground up—a "grammar" rather than a vocabulary (Bernilla-Silva, 2001).

These features of CRT point to facets of schools and schooling that need to be made visible to White prospective teachers, who typically have given little thought to the life experiences of minoritized groups (Ewing, 2018). One of the key practices of CRT that works to make visible the racial inequities of society is the use of *counter-narrative* in the quest for social justice. Recognition of the value of counter-narrative—often called counter-stories or counter-storytelling—in social justice efforts is not new, nor did it begin with the formal development of CRT within the field of Critical Legal Studies in the late 1960s (Miller et al., 2020, pp. 271–272). From the early history of anti-racist endeavors, telling the stories of minoritized people has been an important tool in forcing a caesura in the master narrative of White supremacy, bringing out the lived experience of minoritized people as they strive for freedom, justice, and recognition (Brown, 2010). According to Taylor (2016), people of color "…have first-hand knowledge, as well as multigenerational experience, of the political, social, historical and persistent disadvantages of not being White" (p. 4). For example, African American thinkers writing in the early twentieth century such as W.E.B. Du Bois, Zora Neale Hurston, Fenton Johnson, Carter G. Woodson, and many others explicitly worked to present the voices and experiences of Black Americans both as a form of justice in and of itself and as a way to challenge White supremacy in the age of Jim Crow.

Among CRT scholars and educators, critical storytelling has been an important means to document how race influences the educational experiences of people of color, whose stories counter the stories of the privileged that are considered "normal." As Delgado and Stefancic (2013) noted, "our social world, with its rules, practices, and assignments of prestige and power, is not fixed; rather, we construct it with words, stories, and silence. ... By writing and speaking against them, we may hope to contribute to a better, fairer world" (p. 3). Yosso (2006) states that "counterstories challenge social and racial injustice by listening to and learning from experiences of racism and resistance, despair and hope at the margins of society" (171). Counter-narrative is also powerful to disrupt dominance and privilege; acknowledging the social construction of reality and providing an alternate construction has obvious social and even psychological value for members of minoritized communities (Delgado, 1989). Counter-narrative has also been successfully used by researchers and activists to give voice to the complex, varied and persistent nature of racism on the lived experiences of people of color (Chapman 2007; Parker & Lynn 2002; Yosso 2005). However, the use of counter-narrative in preparing White teachers for teaching students of color does not seem as common, either as a generalized pedagogical tool in teacher preparation or as a specific strategy to address the assumptions White prospective teachers have regarding racism and then springboard the resulting insights for transformative learning. In other words, there is a potential benefit to employing strategies of counter-narrative in an overall praxis of teacher education that is not being realized. Nevertheless, it is important to note that sharing counter-narratives as part of teacher education cannot be the end goal. Rather, counter-narratives, as with theory, should inform intervention in teacher education programs, leading teacher educators and prospective teachers alike to alternative solutions that can be implemented for anti-racist teaching and evaluated in terms of the desired outcomes (Dixson & Rousseau, 2005; Grant, 2009; Miller et al., 2020).

A Critical Race Theory of education should be integrated into teacher education programs as an overarching framework to help preservice teachers understand race as the central construct for analyzing school inequity and for deciphering "the social-structural and cultural significance of race in education" (Ladson-Billings & Tate, 1995, p. 50), particularly the education debt (Ladson-Billings, 2006) that results from both historical and on-going race-based disparities in educational resources and opportunities. Ladson-Billings and Tate (1995) argued that although gender and class intersect with race, explanations based on class and gender differences are not powerful enough to explain all the difference in school experience and performance. This includes but is not limited to higher dropout rates, higher rates of out-of-school discipline, and the so-called failure of Black and Brown students (Welch, et al., 2022). CRT reveals that schools are designed to protect White economic interests through disparate educational opportunities (Ladson-Billings & Tate, 1995).

CRT prioritizes the experience of minoritized communities of color over that of White teachers, even in the branches of CRT that are specifically concerned with the concepts and mechanisms of Whiteness (such as Critical Whiteness Theory). From the standpoint of CRT, educational institutions and practices as currently constituted function to perpetuate White supremacy. The goal of teacher education should be to enable prospective teachers to recognize, acknowledge, and change those institutions and practices. This can be achieved by using history and lived experiences as *counternarratives* (Miller et al., 2020). Counternarratives may be used to support prospective teachers in analyzing the historical practices of slavery and the appropriation of the bodies and labor of enslaved people, the annexing of indigenous lands and the genocide of its original inhabitants (Bauer, 2022; Sabzalian et al., 2021), the dehumanizing of immigrants, the segregation and resegregation of students of color, and current unjust practices such as defunding schools in communities of color and over-disciplining students of color to push them into the carceral system.

2.5   The Vehicle for Transformation: Culturally Relevant and Sustaining Community-Based Teacher Education

CRT, with its emphasis on the ubiquity (and hence centrality) of the lived experience of racism, and its reliance on counter-narrative as both a source of knowledge and a mechanism for critique, should be placed at the center of community-based teacher education that deploys culturally relevant and sustaining pedagogy (Ladson-Billings, 2014; Paris, 2012; Paris & Alim, 2017). This must be done in deep collaboration with local communities of color. Most approaches to preparing White teachers for diverse student populations discussed so far assume a "traditional," university-based teacher education model. However, there are approaches to preparing teachers for diverse students that do not assume a university-centric teacher education program. There are those that draw upon ideas related to community-based learning in an effort to address the needs of communities of color (Ball, 1995; Graue, 2005; Graue & Brown, 2003). As Graue (2005) observes, "there are significant discrepancies in perceptions between school people and parents about school efforts and family involvement in education" (p. 158). These are further exacerbated by racial and cultural differences between poor parents of color and the largely White middle class teacher corps (Bryk & Schneider, 2002; Meier, 2002; Noguera, 2001).

Baquedano-López et al. (2013) revealed in their historical analysis that current education reform and practice regarding parent involvement has been dominated by a discourse incorporating White middle-class values, seeing parents from minoritized communities as problems in need of remedy. This deficit view fails to address the experiences of many parents and students from nondominant backgrounds through intersectional lenses of race, class, and immigration, exhorting non-dominant families to abide by White, middle-class values and expectations. When nondominant families do not meet these expectations, educators consider them uninterested in their children's education and thus blame them for the school's failure to educate their children (Ishimaru et al., 2019).

Zeichner et al. (2016) suggested that addressing these problems requires that teachers know about the communities in which their students grow, develop respectful and trusting relations with students' families and other adults in their communities, and make use of this knowledge and these relationships to support their students' learning (p. 277). Murrell (2000) called this type of teacher a "community teacher" who,

> develops the contextualized knowledge of culture, community, and identity of children and their families as the core of their teaching practice. Community teachers possess the "multicultural competence" they need for accomplished practice in the communities they teach. Community teachers are individuals who typically live and work in the same under-resourced urban neighborhoods and communities where students from diverse backgrounds live and go to school. (p. 340)

In order to implement community-based teacher education, Baquedano-López et al. (2013) argued that teachers need a paradigm shift from seeing parents as a deficit to parents having agency to advocate for their children and resist inequity. This is a type of teacher-family-community collaboration that Zeichner et al. (2016) termed "teacher-family-community solidarity" (p. 278). Solidarity-oriented community-based teacher education has been implemented through community panels involving parents, community leaders as panelists (Zeichner et al., 2016), engaging community members as mentors for prospective teachers (Guillen & Zeichner, 2018; Zeichner et al., 2016; Zygmunt et al., 2018a), and facilitating community and teacher educators in co-constructing teacher education programs (Ball et al., 2023; Fickel et al., 2018; Zeichner et al., 2016). These approaches represent a more democratic and transformative framework of teacher education that decenter the power of teacher educators and deconstruct the traditional White curriculum of teacher education programs by integrating the cultures, experiences, and practices of communities of color.

Restructuring teacher education from the standpoint of community-based learning is predicated on the belief "in the educability of all students, thus providing students from different social backgrounds, with diverse levels of ability and behavioral dispositions, opportunities to learn and live together" (Lopez et al., 2012, p. 23). Aiming toward social justice and equity for minoritized students and communities, community-based teacher education, on the one hand, has proved effective for preparing White preservice teachers to teach in diverse communities (Guillen & Zeichner, 2018; Zeichner et al., 2016; Zygmunt et al., 2018a, 2018b). On the other hand, community-based teacher education has the potential to encourage teacher education programs to actively recruit, prepare, and retain teachers of color from and for minoritized communities. The combination, then, of community-based teacher education informed by CRT and employing culturally relevant and sustaining pedagogy holds promise to dismantle the institutional and societal attitudes and practices of deficit thinking and a savior mentality toward marginalized students and communities.

2.6   THE ENGINE FOR TRANSFORMATION: CRITICAL REFLECTION AND GENERATIVE CHANGE FOR TRANSFORMATIVE ACTION

As critiqued earlier, teacher education practice and research tend to focus on changing prospective teachers' attitudes and perceptions based on their self-reported evidence; there is a lack of focus on prospective teachers' classroom actions. In order to support prospective teachers in bridging reflection with action we argue here that critical reflection for transformative learning and generative change are the ideal engine for community-based teacher education.

Critical reflection is a hermeneutic approach to individual learning going back at least to Donald Schon (1983), if not John Dewey (1933). It involves repeated reexamination of one's assumptions about knowledge and understanding, particularly those that are socially, politically, or culturally based. However, as Ball (2012) insisted in her AERA Presidential Address, knowing is not enough: there must be a movement from thinking to action and from critique to intervention. For example, Brookfield (1995) argued that "reflection in and of itself is not enough; it must always be linked to how the world can be changed" (p. 217). This is a position that resonates with Mezirow's (1990) idea that critical reflection is necessary for changing both how teachers teach and learners learn. He termed this *transformative learning* and emphasized that "reflective discourse and its resulting insights alone do not make for transformative learning. Acting upon these emancipatory insights, a praxis is also necessary" (p. 354). Furthermore, that praxis requires goals which, in the context of preparing teachers for minoritized and oppressed student populations must rest in anti-racist teaching for educational equity. Otherwise the "emancipatory insights" of critical reflection, no matter how important to the individual, cannot translate to collaborative action for community benefit. According to Freire (1970), the solution is not to "integrate" the oppressed "into the structure of oppression" but to transform the structure so that the oppressed can become "beings for themselves" (p. 61). Accordingly, Liu (2015) links the practice of critical reflection with the goal of transformative action for social justice, defining critical reflection as

> a process of constantly analyzing, questioning, and critiquing established assumptions of oneself, schools, and the society about teaching and learning, and the social and political implications of schooling, and implementing changes to previous actions that have been supported by those established assumptions for the purpose of supporting student learning and a better schooling and more [just] society for all children. (pp. 10–11)

Liu (2015) articulated a full processual model of critical reflection for transformative learning based on Brookfield's work. This model includes a cycle of six steps of assumption analysis, contextual awareness, imaginative speculation, reflective skepticism, reflection-based action, and reflection on reflection-based action (See Liu, 2015, p. 148 for a detailed description of the six steps). Building on Liu (2015) and situated in our earlier argument for community-based teacher education, we further argue that educators need to gain knowledge and skills from the students, families, and members of the minoritized community in order to modify the reflection-informed solutions and implement their reflection-based actions. Teaching and learning grounded on the funds of knowledge (Gonzalez, et al., 2005) of minoritized communities can make transformative impacts on these students. For example, the more than decade-long community-based teacher education program at Ball State University (Zygmunt et al., 2018a, 2018b) demonstrates the power to prepare the "development of culturally responsive teachers" while "furthering the priorities of the communities in which candidates work" (p. 130). We therefore modify Liu's six-stage framework by adding one stage of community-based learning between reflective skepticism and reflection-based action. Figure 2.2 provides a visual representation of the seven-stage hermeneutic cycle of critical reflection for transformative learning.

Critical reflection can effect changes at the classroom level, but what about the larger institutional changes that are also necessary for anti-racist education? Here we turn to generativity for an answer. Generativity is the generation of new or novel behavior in problem solving (Epstein, 1996). It is a complex psychosocial construct that describes how an individual responds to societal demands, inner desires, conscious concerns, beliefs, and commitments. The concept includes productivity and creativity to make the world a better place. It also manifests as a concern for one's legacy that leads to concrete goals and transformative action.

Research on generativity over the past seven decades suggests that generativity is a formal, predictive theory of creative behavior or activity on the part of individuals. Ball (2009), noting that teachers are faced with societal demands to which they must respond creatively, proposed that generativity provides a framework explaining the process by which teachers engage in transformative change of the classroom lives of diverse student populations. Given that nearly 40% of teachers entering the classroom report feeling unprepared for the challenges that await them, generativity could also guide teacher educators in their transformation of program practices. Ball (2009) thus combined generative theory and teacher efficacy in a model designed to prepare teachers who believe in their potential ability to affect positive change in the lives of their students and who also think in generative ways that result in transformative action in their classrooms. Ball's model of generative change includes four stages facilitating teachers' development of a change-oriented mindset, prompting metacognitive awareness, a sense of agency, a sense of advocacy, and the

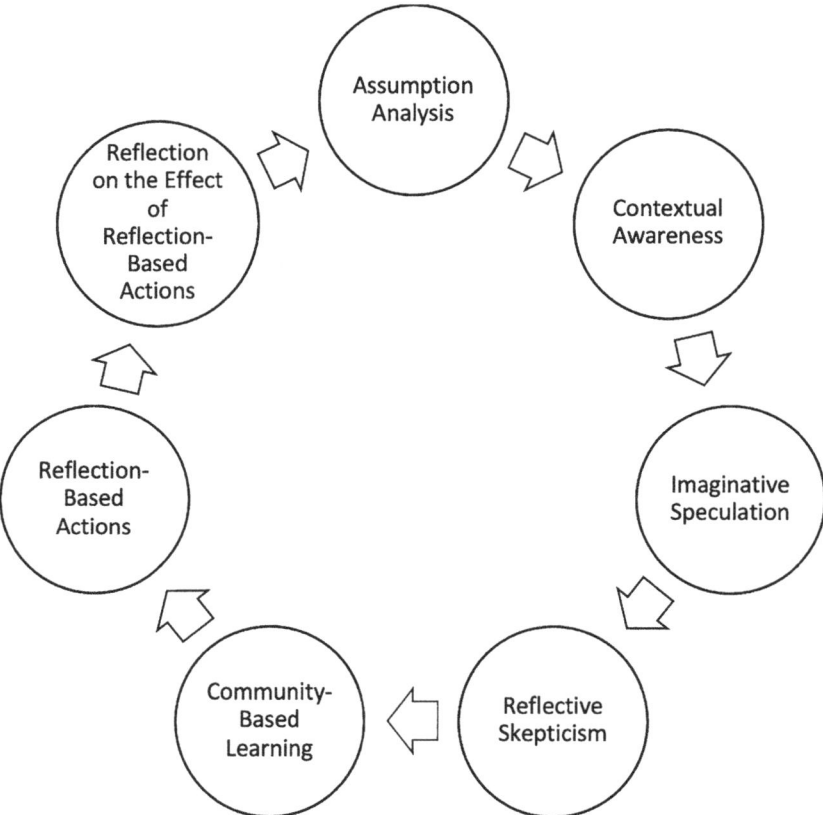

Fig. 2.2 The hermeneutic cycle of critical reflection for transformative learning. Adapted from Liu (2015, p. 148)

development of a personal voice concerning the education of diverse students. Figure 2.3 (below) illustrates Ball's model as a series of steps by which individuals move from metacognitive awakening to their own sense of efficacy for becoming transformative intellectuals (Giroux, 1988) able to reshape curriculum, pedagogy, institutional structures, and classroom practices. The result is the preparation of teachers who are agents of change rather than objects of change, forging new relationships between teachers and students, schools and communities.

In the context of preparing teachers for anti-racist teaching via community-based teacher education, the first task is to infuse the steps of

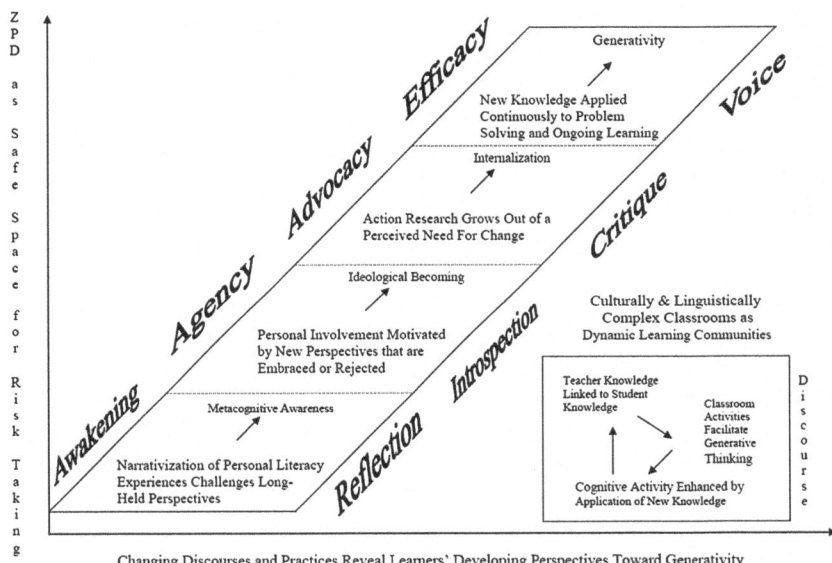

Fig. 2.3 Model of generative change: the processes through which teachers and students develop voice, generativity, and efficacy in their thinking and practice (Ball, 2009, p. 66)

critical reflection with insight from CRT, and second to ensure systematic movement from analyzing distorted assumptions and obtaining critical awareness to generating new knowledge and taking action to transform learning undertaken in collaboration by both education professionals and the students and families in the community. Combining this collaborative process with CRT provides two vital affordances to community-based teacher education. First, it provides clear guidance for all parties in identifying racism afflicting the educational system and actively searching for anti-racist teaching alternatives to the ways in which students and families are failed by our current educational systems. Second, the frameworks of critical reflection for transformative learning and generative change, when adopted collaboratively by educators and communities, can help all parties generate new knowledge and develop into transformative intellectuals (Ball, 2009; Giroux, 1988). According to Ball (2009), knowledge becomes generative "when the teacher continues that learning by making connections with his or her students' knowledge and needs and begins planning the teaching based on what he or she is learning" (p. 48).

Finally, critical reflection for transformative learning and generative change provides a valuable framework for teacher educators to conduct research on the content of and procedures for prospective teachers' reflection on teaching a diverse body of students (see, for example, Ball, 2009; Ball et al., 2023; Liu, 2015, 2020; Liu, et al., 2017; Liu & Ball, 2019). It further provides a critical lens to guide teacher educators to conduct research on the real actions of prospective teachers in their teaching—whether or not their reflection brings about transformative and generative actions in anti-racist teaching. Research based on prospective teachers' classroom actions that goes beyond depending solely on written reflections can help teacher educators gain a better understanding of how to improve their own support for prospective teachers to achieve transformative learning in anti-racist teaching. Therefore, the frameworks, on the one hand, point out the importance of focusing on prospective teachers' teaching practices and, on the other hand, guide teacher educators to analyze prospective teachers' actions to determine whether or not they are transformative in terms of teaching diverse learners.

However, our use of the framework is not only to guide research but also to inform pedagogy and curriculum: just as teachers themselves must use the fruit of critical reflection to transform their teaching practices, so too must teacher educators use theoretical and research insights to ground transformation of teacher education practices. It should be clear by now that the framework for our research and teaching relies on developing knowledge of the preservice teachers, students and their communities—the funds of knowledge all parties can bring to schools and schooling. Therefore, before continuing with the findings of our research and the recommendations and programming stemming from those findings, we will briefly summarize the methods we used to design and conduct our research, and describe the institutions, participants, and communities in which the research occurred.

2.7   About This Research

This longitudinal qualitative study (Saldana, 2013) lasted over a decade from 2008 until 2019, spanning three teacher education programs in two states in the United States. Creswell (2005) stated that longitudinal research involves the survey procedure of collecting data about trends with the same population, changes in a cohort group or subpopulation, or changes in a panel group of the same individuals over time. Thus, in longitudinal designs, the participants may be different people or the same people. (p. 357)

Longitudinal studies explore change in "substance and form, content and process" (Hargreaves et al., 2001, p. 184) over time. Thus, as Saldana (2013) argued, a qualitative study should not be labeled by the researchers as longitudinal "solely on the basis of extended time in the field or due to an extended period of time between pre- and post-interviews" (p. 3). Instead, researchers need to take into account three factors (p. 5):

- Considerations of how time interacts and interplays with the collection and analysis of qualitative data;
- Attention to the multiple and the possible types of change; and
- The inferences and effects on human actions and participant world views.

Time plays an invaluable role in our own journey to become teacher educators and researchers. As Compton-Lilly (2012, 2016, 2020) demonstrated powerfully in her decade-long longitudinal studies of children's literacy practices, time is an integral dimension of people's identity construction that impacts how they make sense of their worlds. This is true to both research participants and the researchers. In the context of this book, time plays a vital role in participating teachers' learning to become teachers. As such, one important focus of the analysis reported in this book is prospective teachers' changes/or not in their assumptions and teaching practices during their journey of learning to teach. Longitudinal qualitative studies are thus observational over an extensive period of time. As Saldaña (2003) described, during this time, the researcher focuses on

how people think, feel, and act from moment through moment to capture in-depth perceptions and meanings, to extract stories from narrative inquiry, and to log rich details for individual biography. Additionally, we learn how human actions and participant perceptions might change during the course of a study to reveal temporal-based themes and patterns of human development or social process. (p. 4)

Saldaña (2003) continued to articulate that the concept of change is a complicated one as change is related to time and "since time is contextual and our social actions and circumstances in it are contextual, change is contextual" (p. 9). Although Saldaña (2003) agreed with Pettigrew (1990) that researchers should define the meaning of change in each longitudinal study and how change will be inferred and observed before, during, and after the analysis, he also pointed out the importance of being aware of the particular conditions of the particular fields of study. In the context of our study, we defined change as seen in participants' habits of mind regarding race and racism and their patterns of acting in interacting with minoritized students. Guided by our theoretical framework and our previous experiences in teaching prospective teachers, we understand that prospective teachers might be able to demonstrate change in their perceptions about race and racism but their perceptual changes do not necessarily lead to changes in their actions in teaching minoritized students. As such, in our definition of change, it encompasses changes in beliefs and perceptions, but more importantly, changes in actions. Processes linking changes in perception to action include stages explained earlier in the framework, such as assumption analysis, contextual awareness, imaginative speculation, reflective skepticism, community-based learning, reflection-based action, and reflection on the effects of reflection-based action. At the same time, we kept open the possibility that habits of mind and patterns of acting could change at different rates or in different ways over time for the same participant as well as among different participants in different teacher education programs situated in their specific social, cultural, and political contexts.

The data collection portion of the longitudinal study reported in this book ran from 2008 to 2019 and included participants from three different teacher education programs in three different state public universities located in two states in the United States. Major participants included seven White prospective teachers and two prospective teachers of color and their classroom mentor teachers, who were all White. We followed the prospective teachers for two to four academic semesters, interviewing each of them two to three times a semester, and collected their written reflections as well. Over the span of their participation, we also observed their classroom teaching multiple times, paying special attention to their classroom practices, especially regarding their habits of mind and patterns of acting regarding race and racism. Specifically, we worked to understand connections between their habits of mind and patterns of acting, keeping in mind that there could be disparities between what they said in interviews and written reflections, and in the behaviors we observed in the classroom over time.

Time is also an inseparable factor that has shaped our identities as teacher educators and researchers over the decade of teaching, researching, supervising, and collaborating. Over the years, the three of us have collaborated through conference presentations, teaching, and writing with a joint interest in how to better prepare future teachers for an increasingly diverse student population. We repeatedly explored the question of the habits of mind and patterns of acting of prospective teachers in different teacher education programs situated in different institutions, paying special attention to how different program designs, requirements, and cultures contextualize prospective teacher' habits of mind and patterns of acting. At the same time, we made efforts to implement pedagogical tools and strategies informed by our research into our own practice as teacher educators and researchers.

2.7.1 Study Context

This study was situated in three different elementary teacher education programs: the undergraduate elementary education programs of a large flagship state university in the Midwest (here called Midwestern University), a small state university in the same Midwestern state (here called Clear Lake University), and an elementary alternative route to licensure (ARL) program in a state university in the Southwest (here called Desert View University). The diversity of institutions and settings and the span of 12 years in this study are important elements to our argument concerning the widespread nature of the habits of mind and patterns of acting we discuss in this book, as such we will take a moment to briefly describe each institution and their locations. We adopted Milner's (2012) urban education framework defining three types of urban education contexts—urban intensive, urban emergent, and urban characteristic—to categorize the contexts of the three teacher education programs. A critical aspect of Milner's framework lies in the importance of recognizing and acknowledging the multigenerational racism and the opportunity gaps that students in urban schools suffer as the root cause of their learning outcomes. However, educators often deny the historical and current realities, blaming students and families for the "problems" in a school or district. Milner (2012) described that truancy, lack of motivation, parents' lack of involvement all were "urban" problems that extended beyond the administration, leadership at the district office, or teachers. For the leaders in the district, the problems in the district were with the students themselves. "Tell us, Professor Milner, what we need to do to control the students (and their parents)" was the message I received. (pp. 557–558)

Milner pointed out that teachers and researchers need to transform the pervading deficit view of students and parents in urban communities to an asset framework: "There is a rich array of excellence, intellect, and talent among the people in urban environments— human capital that makes meaningful contributions to the very fabric of the human condition in the United States and abroad" (p. 558). Milner further called for educators to stop blaming students and families in the urban communities, acknowledge their own role in creating and perpetuating inequities in their schools, and actively implement anti-racist teaching to create equitable learning opportunities that minoritized students have long been denied. It is through this critical lens we describe the contexts of the teacher education programs we studied.

2.8   MIDWESTERN UNIVERSITY

Midwestern University is the flagship campus for a land-grant state system of (at the time of this research) more than 20 campuses, 11 of which produced some combination of undergraduate and graduate degrees, including teacher education. As with many state university systems, some of the campuses began as normal schools, only becoming comprehensive universities during the second half of the twentieth century. Midwestern University itself, however, began in the mid-nineteenth century as a comprehensive university and remains the flagship campus in the system, in part because of its size (approximately one quarter of all the students in the state system) and in part because of the wealth and resources it has amassed through research, grantsmanship, sports-focused alumni donations, and patent management. The city in which Midwestern University is located (and therefore the school district in which our participants were placed) has over 250,000 people in a metropolitan area of more than half a million, making the schools in the district urban emergent—located in a city with fewer than one million residents—based on Milner's (2012) urban school classifications. Milner (2012) points out that, although schools in urban emergent districts are located in smaller cities, they mirror the diversity in the student demographics found in larger, urban intensive districts. In this case, according to the National Center for Education Statistics (NCES, 2023), students of color represented 53% of the total student population in the district, although overall the metropolitan area was 90% White. Much of the rhetoric of "failing schools" in the district thus focused on the minoritized populations, blaming them for academic and social troubles.

The five-semester elementary education program at Midwestern emphasized preparing future reflective practitioners able to foster high academic achievement in all students, especially those with diverse racial, cultural, linguistic, and socioeconomic backgrounds. To be admitted to the program as juniors, students had to demonstrate multicultural and reflective competence in their admission materials. Once in the program, there were numerous opportunities for prospective teachers to study multicultural education and teaching for social justice and equity, and to put those ideas into practice through field experiences. Each of the first four semesters included a practicum: one on community experiences, one on literacy, one on math and arts, and another on social studies, science, PE, and music. Student teaching occurred in the fifth semester. Practicum and student teaching experiences were coordinated and supervised under a *clinical triad* model (Lombardi, 2001) in which the prospective teacher worked in a real classroom under the guidance of a mentor teacher and a university-based supervisor.

Courses included a required introduction discussing diversity, multicultural education, and reflective teaching using Grant and Sleeter (2007) and Zeichner and Liston (1996) as well as guest talks by university specialists in those approaches. Two of the eight methods courses were taught by faculty who had made significant contributions to multicultural education and CRT. There were also upper-level electives on US education that dealt with discrimination and segregation. The remaining methods courses were primarily taught by doctoral students. All participants in this study took a course stressing CRT and culturally responsive teaching during their fourth semester. Finally, field supervisors—almost all doctoral students—conducted periodic observations, held debriefings, both individually with the prospective teachers and in tandem with the cooperating teacher, and held weekly seminars in which they discussed readings as well as attempted to engage students in reflecting on their field experiences.

Throughout their degree program, prospective teachers were required to upload reflections into an online ePortfolio, starting with their autobiography and teaching philosophy, and then addressing their teaching and learning experiences with the goal of showing fulfillment of the state and program teaching standards and fealty to the program's core values. Prospective teachers were encouraged to modify their autobiography and teaching philosophy statements each semester, but the primary focus was on demonstrating their teaching and learning with lesson plans, reflections, and supporting materials. During the fifth semester of student teaching, prospective teachers kept a reflective journal that was regularly reviewed and commented upon by their supervisors but was not included in their ePortfolio. By the end of the fifth semester, prospective teachers were expected to assemble their artifacts in their ePortfolio to demonstrate their fulfillment of the standards. Their ePortfolio was then evaluated and used as a performance assessment for licensure recommendation by their teacher education program.

2.9   CLEAR LAKE UNIVERSITY

Clear Lake University is another campus in the same system as Midwestern, but located in a rural town with a year-round population of around 15,000 situated some 45 miles from the Midwestern campus in an area of rich farmland. When we conducted data collection, the town itself was overwhelmingly White (88% according to the 2010 census), but had a significant Latinx population (a little over 9%), primarily families of farm and factory workers of Mexican origin. There were clear divisions between the White and Latinx communities with the city's power structure effectively closed to the non-White population. The Latinx families primarily lived in the two trailer parks on the outskirts of town, segregated from the White community. The K-12 schools were a primary point of contact between the two communities. The student population in the school district was more diverse than the population as a whole: White students were about 58% of the total student population, Latinx students accounted for approximately 34% and Black students about 3%; contrary to the student diversity, the teacher corps was nearly 100% White, with only one Latinx teacher in the entire district at the time of our study (NCES, 2023). Clear Lake School District matched Milner's (2012) identification of urban characteristic schools that "are not located in big cities but may be beginning to experience increases in challenges that are sometimes associated with urban contexts such as an increase in English language learners in a community" (p. 570). The White teacher corps in the district indeed demonstrated deficit attitudes toward Latinx students and their families, and in some cases expressed jealousy over the "special privileges" they perceived those students and families receiving, such as free bus passes for parents to attend parent-teacher events (many of whom, as undocumented immigrants, could not legally drive).

The Clear Lake teacher education program drew students from every part of the state, the majority of them White women from rural or suburban locales. Because of relatively strong links between the teacher education program at Midwestern and that at Clear Lake, and of course shared external elements such as state teacher licensure standards, many of the details of the two teacher education programs were quite similar, including the requirement for regular reflection and the use of the clinical supervision model for practicum and student teaching placements. However, there was no field placement specifically designed for community engagement for prospective teachers. When the data was collected at Clear Lake University (between 2011 and 2015), most prospective teachers in the elementary education program were required to compose a paper portfolio to document their teaching and learning; faculty members who supervised the practicum and student teaching had the freedom to use some digital form of portfolio. Unlike prospective teachers in the elementary program in Midwestern University, who had four practicum semesters before their student teaching, prospective teachers in Clear Lake had only two practicum semesters before student teaching. Also, unlike supervision at Midwestern, supervision at Clear Lake was the responsibility of faculty, not graduate students. As a teaching-oriented university located in a rural part of the state, each faculty member was in charge of supervising many prospective teachers during their student teaching semester, conducting four observations of each prospective teacher. Normally, faculty had a teaching load of four courses per semester; supervising four to five student teachers during the student teaching semester was considered to be one course load. Since rural school districts (and schools) tend to be relatively small, a faculty member's observation visits could be spread over a 75-mile radius around the university campus, which limited the opportunities for informal, unannounced observations. One interesting difference between Midwestern and Clear Lake is that mentor teachers at Clear Lake received training when they first agreed to serve, a one-semester course taught by teacher education faculty. Mentor teachers at Midwestern were not trained for their role.

2.10   DESERT VIEW UNIVERSITY

Desert View University is one of two main campuses of a state system in the Southwestern United States, situated in a large, highly diverse city of nearly 2.5 million people. A recent addition to the Carnegie list of R1 universities, Desert View was transitioning from a teaching-focused mission to one emphasizing research. At the same time, the university was proud of its service to the local community (75% of the students in Desert View come from the surrounding metropolitan area). The 2010 census reported the local metropolitan area is majority-minority, with 42% of the population identifying as White, 28% Latinx, 11% Black, 12% Asian, and more than a third non-native English speakers. The local school district, which was coterminal with the entire metropolitan area, was one of the largest in the United States and even more diverse than the population as a whole, with 47% of the student population identifying as Latinx, 21% White, 15% Black, 6% Asian or Asian American, less than 2% Native Hawaiian or Other Pacific Islander, 0.3% American Indian or Alaska Natives (NCES, 2023). The Desert View School District demonstrates the feature of urban intensive—a district located in a city with more than one million residents (Milner, 2012). However, the teacher corps was considerably Whiter (73%) than either the student population or the general population (NCES, 2023); as the district had a system of neighborhood schools the demographics of which closely tracked those of the surrounding neighborhood, some schools in the district had a student population almost entirely non-White, and a teaching staff that was primarily White. Moreover, because so much of the population of the metropolitan area originated from outside the United States, a large portion of the student population was ELLs, with dozens of native languages spoken in the students' homes. There were, therefore, several special funding lines for schools with higher rates of low-SES students, or high numbers of ELL students, in addition to Federal Title I program funds. As in Clear Lake school district, these funding lines were regarded with some jealousy by White teachers, particularly those serving in non-Title I schools. The district made little effort to support non-English speakers except through deficit-oriented ESL pullout classes, justifying this lack of support in terms of the dizzying numbers of languages spoken at home.

Unlike the research participants from two undergraduate elementary programs in Midwestern University and Clear Lake University, the participants at Desert View were in a non-traditional and alternative route to licensure (ARL) elementary education program. This program was designed for students already holding a bachelor's degree in some area other than education, and thus could be completed in a much shorter time than a traditional teacher education degree. Unlike the Midwestern University students, who had the opportunity to take multiple courses related to Critical Race Theory and multicultural education and a community engagement practicum semester, students in the ARL program were required to take one multicultural course. As with the other two teacher education programs in this study, the program at Desert View employed an ePortfolio system, and used a clinical triad model for prospective teacher supervision. Unlike the other two institutions, however, there was much less emphasis on producing reflective practitioners. Rather, the majority of the program descriptions, course materials, and so forth focused on the use of the ePortfolio to document dispositions and classroom achievements. The selection of clinical supervisors at Desert View was also different from either of the other two institutions: Supervisors at Desert View were neither graduate students (as at Midwestern) nor faculty (as at Clear Lake), but independent contractors, mostly retired White public school teachers from the district. Mentor teachers were mostly White as well. Clinical supervisors and mentor teachers were both overseen by a permanent staff member of the university, and not directly by faculty. Due to the isolation of the city (a five-hour drive from the next largest metropolitan area), the size of the school district, and a perpetual shortage of teachers in the district, Desert View University students were always placed in the local school district, either in traditional public or charter schools. The student body of the undergraduate teacher education program at Desert View, although more diverse than the national average, was Whiter than the K-12 student population in the district, but slightly more diverse than the district's teacher corps.

2.10.1   Participants, Data Sources, and Analysis

For this study, we recruited seven White prospective teachers and two prospective teachers of color from the three teacher education programs described above as the primary participants. In Midwest University where this research first took place, we started by analyzing 20 White prospective teachers' written reflections to help us establish a general understanding of prospective teachers' habits of mind. We then recruited three White female prospective teachers (Ella, Judy, and Karla, all pseudonyms) as the primary participants for a four-semester long study (Fall 2008–Spring 2010), starting from their third semester of practicum through their fourth semester practicum, fifth semester student teaching, and a follow-up after their student teaching. We also interviewed some of their teacher educators and their classroom mentor teachers. At Clear Lake University, we recruited two White female prospective teachers (Cathy and Abby, also pseudonyms) as the primary participants (Fall 2012–Spring 2013). At Desert View University, the participants included one White female prospective teacher Helen, one White male prospective teacher Craig, one Black male prospective teacher (Jevon) and one Latina female prospective teacher (Sophia) in the research (all pseudonyms; Spring 2018–Fall 2019). Since the research reported in this book focuses on the habits of mind and patterns of acting of White prospective teachers, we will use findings from the two prospective teachers of color primarily in Chaps. 6 and 7 to demonstrate some examples of what prospective teachers were able to do when they used their racialized experiences to inform their teaching.

In order to answer our research questions on White prospective teachers' habits of mind regarding race and racism and their patterns of acting dealing with race and racism in their teaching, we adopted data triangulation (Creswell, 2013), a process of "collecting information from a diverse range of individuals and settings using a variety of methods" (Maxwell, 2013, p. 128) to develop a comprehensive understanding of the complexity and intertwined relationship between prospective teachers' saying and doing. Specifically, we collected participants' written reflections to find out how they talked about race and racism. We then triangulated their written reflections with interviews and intensive classroom observations. The interviews made use of a standard set of initial questions at the beginning of each semester regarding the participants' teaching philosophy and their goals related to teaching for equity for the semester, and then revisited those questions at the end of each semester. For example, common questions for all the interviews included "How has your semester been so far?" and "What were your overall goals related to teaching for equity this semester?" We allowed the conversations to evolve organically from there, in some cases initiating a line of questions drawn from their written reflections or our observations. Classroom observations focused on how the participants interacted with their students, especially the students of color, and how they dealt with issues related to race and racism. We paid special attention to whether or not they implemented actions and strategies they talked about in their written reflections.

For participants in Midwestern University, we included their written reflections over three semesters, interviewed each of the three primary participants six times and observed each of them four times in a span of four-semesters. For participants in Clear Lake University, we included their written reflections in two semesters, interviewed each of the two participants four times and observed each of them four times over two semesters. Finally, for the participants in Desert View, we included their written reflections in one semester, interviewed each of the four participants twice and observed each of them three times in a span of three semesters. Table 2.1 summarizes the participants (identified by pseudonyms) and data sources. The length of each interview was at least an hour. The length of the observations varied, depending on the lessons being observed. Sometimes, one observation ran as long as an entire morning or an entire afternoon with the efforts to understand the classroom realities as much as possible.

Our data analysis of the written reflections, interviews, and classroom observations primarily consisted of *a priori* coding (Saldaña, 2013), using our theoretical framework to code for patterns in the data. *A priori* coding

Table 2.1 Participants and data sources

Institution	Primary participants' pseudonyms	Participants' race/ethnicity/ gender	ePortfolio reflection/ written reflection	Interview	Observation
Midwestern University	Ella	White, female	Three semesters	Six times	Four times
	Judy	White, female	Three semesters	Six times	Four times
	Karla	White, female	Three semesters	Six times	Four times
Clearwater University	Cathy	White, female	Two semesters	Four times	Four times
	Abby	White, female	Two semesters	Four times	Four times
Desert View University	Helen	White, female	One semester	Two times	Three times
	Craig	White, male	One semester	Two times	Three times
	Jevon	Black, male	One semester	Two times	Three times
	Sofia	Latina, female	One semester	Two times	Three times

of prospective teachers' written reflections and interviews, guided by CRT, helped us identify their habits of mind regarding race, racism, and educational inequity. Similarly, *a priori* coding of the same data guided by the framework of critical reflection and generativity for transformative learning enabled us to analyze the critical nature and transformative potential of participants' reflection. Finally, *a priori* coding of our transcriptions and notes on classroom observations, guided by both frameworks, made it possible for us to compare participants' habits of mind with the patterns of acting they demonstrated in the classroom. All three sets of findings then informed not only the application of our research theories and methods, but also the efficacy of our teacher education curriculum and pedagogy.

2.11   Conclusion

With this understanding of our theoretical framework and the context in which we conducted our research, we turn to our findings on White preservice teachers' habits of mind regarding race and racism. Chap. 3, "From Camouflage to Pledging Commitment," begins by summarizing Jack Mezirow's notion of *habits of mind* and the ways in which it dovetails with related concepts from scholars of critical reflection, such as Stephen D. Brookfield and Max van Manen. Then we delve into the data from our research with White preservice teachers, identifying common habits of mind in their written and spoken reflections, setting up Chap. 4 on White preservice teachers' patterns of acting.

References

Anderson, L. M., & Stillman, J. A. (2013). Student teaching's contribution to preservice teacher development: A review of research focused on the preparation of teachers for urban and high-needs contexts. *Review of Educational Research, 83*(1), 3–69.

Aptheker, H. (1975). Some introductory remarks: The history of anti-racism in the United States. *The Black Scholar, 6*(5), 16–22.

Aptheker, H. (1992). *Anti-racism in U.S. history: The first two hundred years.* Greenwood Press.

Arneback, E. (2022). Becoming an anti-racist teacher: Countering racism in education. *Teachers and Teaching 28*(3) 357–368.

Ball, A. F. (1995). Community-based learning in urban settings as a model for educational reform. *Applied Behavioral Science Review, 3*(2), 127–146.

Ball, A. F. (2009). Toward a theory of generative change in culturally and linguistically complex classrooms. *American Educational Research Journal,* *46*(1), 45–72.

Ball, A. F. (2012). Presidential address: To know is not enough: Knowledge, power, and the zone of generativity. *Educational Researcher Journal,* *41*(8), 283–293.

Ball, A. F., Greene, D. M., Friedman, J. S. L., & Dray, B. J. (2023). The trifecta framework: Preparing agents of change in urban education. *Urban Education,* *58*(9), 1912–1942.

Banks, J. A. (1974). *Multicultural education: In search of definitions and goals.* National Academy of Education.

Banks, J. A. (1995). Multicultural education and curriculum transformation. *The Journal of Negro Education, 64*(4), 390–400.

Banks, J. A., & Banks, C. A. M. (2010). *Multicultural education: Issues and perspectives* (8th ed.). Wiley.

Baquedano-López, P., Alexander, R. A., & Hernandez, S. J. (2013). Equity issues in parental and community involvement in schools: What teacher educators need to know. *Review of Research in Education, 37*(1), 149–182.

Bauer, N. K. (2022). *Tender violence in U.S. schools: Benevolent Whiteness and the dangers of heroic white womanhood.* Routledge.

Berman, P., & McLaughlin, M. W. (1975). *Federal programs supporting educational change, Vol. IV: The findings in review.* Rand.

Bernilla-Silva, E. (2001). *White supremacy and racism in the post-civil rights era.* Lynne Rienner Publishers.

Blum, L. A. (1992). *Antiracism, multiculturalism, and interracial community: Three educational values for a multicultural society. Distinguished lecture series, 1991–1992.* Massachusetts University.

Brookfield, S. A. (1995). *Becoming a critically reflective teacher.* Jossey-Bass.

Brown, A. L. (2010). Counter-memory and race: An examination of African American scholars' challenges to early twentieth century K-12 historical discourses. *The Journal of Negro Education, 79*(1), 54–65.

Brown, K. D. (2014). Teaching in color: A critical race theory in education analysis of the literature on preservice teachers of color and teacher education in the US. *Race Ethnicity and Education, 17*(3), 326–345.

Bryan, N. (2021). *Toward a BlackBoyCrit pedagogy: Black boys, male Teachers, and early childhood classroom practices.* Routledge.

Bryk, A., & Schneider, B. (2002). *Trust in schools: A core resource for improvement.* Russell Sage Foundation.

Bullivant, B. M. (1972). The cultural reality of curriculum development. *Education News, 13*(9), 14–17.

Burant, T. J. (1999). Finding, using, and losing (?) voice: A preservice teacher's experiences in an urban educative practicum. *Journal of Teacher Education, 50*(3), 209–219.

Chapman, T. K. (2007). Interrogating classroom relationships and events: Using portraiture and critical race theory in education research. *Educational Researcher, 36*(3), 156–162.

Cochran-Smith, M., Villegas, A. M., Abrams, L., Chavez-Moreno, L., Mills, T., & Stern, R. (2015). Critiquing teacher preparation research: An overview of the field, part II. *Journal of Teacher Education, 66*(2), 109–121.

Compton-Lilly, C. (2012). *Reading time: The literate lives of urban secondary students and their families*. Teachers College Press.

Compton-Lilly, C. (2016). Time in education: Intertwined dimensions and theoretical possibilities. *Time & Society, 25*(3), 575–593.

Compton-Lilly, C. (2020). *Time in education: Intertwined dimensions and theoretical possibilities*. Garn Press.

Conrad, J., Reisman, A., Patterson, T., Jay, L., Kaplan, A., Eisman, J., & Chan, W. (2023). White preservice teachers facilitating African American history discussions: Tensions of identity in practice. *Teaching and Teacher Education, 125*, 1–11.

Creswell, J. W. (2005). *Educational research: Planning, conducting, and evaluating quantitative and qualitative research*. Pearson.

Creswell, J. W. (2013). *Qualitative inquiry & research design: Choosing among five approaches (3rd ed.)*. SAGE.

Dei, G. J., & James, I. M. (1999). Becoming black. *Race, Ethnicity, and Education, 1*(1), 91–108.

Delgado, R. (1989). Storytelling for oppositionists and others: A plea for narrative. *Michigan Law Review, 87*(8), 2411–2441. https://doi.org/10.2307/1289308

Delgado, R., & Stefancic, J. (2013). *Critical race theory: The cutting edge. 3rd ed.* Temple University Press.

Delgado, R., & Stefancic, J. (2017). *Critical race theory: An introduction* (3rd ed.). NYU Press.

Depalma, R. (2010). Toward a practice of polyphonic dialogue in multicultural teacher education. *Curriculum Inquiry, 40*(3), 436–453.

Dewey, J. (1933). *How we think: A restatement of the relation of reflective thinking to the educative process*. Heath & Co Publishers.

Dixson, A. D., & Rousseau, C. K. (2005). And we are still not saved: Critical race theory in education ten years later. *Race Ethnicity and Education, 8*(1), 7–27.

Earick, M. E. (2009). *Racially equitable teaching: Beyond the whiteness of professional development for early childhood educators*. Peter Lang.

Ellsworth, E. (1989). Why doesn't this feel empowering? Working through the repressive myths of critical pedagogy. *Harvard Educational Review, 59*(3), 298–324.

Epstein, R. (1996). *Cognition, creativity, and behavior: Selected essays*. Praeger.

Evans-Winters, V. E., & Twyman Hoff, P. (2011). The aesthetics of white racism in pre-service teacher education: A critical race theory perspective. *Race Ethnicity and Education, 14*(4), 461–479.

Ewing, E. (2018). *Ghosts in the schoolyard: Racism and school closings on Chicago's South Side*. The University of Chicago Press.

Fickel, L., Abbiss, J., Brown, L., & Astall, C. (2018). The importance of community knowledge in learning to teach: Foregrounding Māori cultural knowledge to support preservice teachers' development of culturally responsive practice. *Peabody Journal of Education, 93*(3), 285–294.

Finn, G. P. T. (1985). Multcultural anti-racism and Scottish education. *Scottish Educational Review, 19*(1), 39–49.

Freire, P. (1970). *Pedagogy of the oppressed*. Translation from the 1968 Portuguese original by Myra Bergman Ramos. Herder and Herder.

Gao, S., Liu, K., & McKinney, M. (2019). Learning formative assessment in the field: Analysis of reflective conversations between preservice teachers and their classroom mentors. *International Journal of Mentoring and Coaching in Education, 8*(3), 197–216.

Gay, G. (1977). Changing conceptions of multicultural education. *Education Perspective, 16*(4), 4–9.

Gay, G. (2000). *Culturally responsive teaching: Theory, research, and practice*. Teachers College Press.

Gay, G. (2002). Preparing for culturally responsive teaching. *Journal of Teacher Education, 53*(2), 106–116.

Gay, G. (2005). Politics of multicultural teacher education. *Journal of Teacher Education, 3*(56), 221–228.

Giroux, H. A. (1988). *Teachers as intellectuals: Toward a critical pedagogy of learning* (Critical studies in education series). Praeger.

Gist, C. D. (2014). *Preparing teachers of color to teach: Culturally responsive teacher education in theory and practice*. Springer.

Gist, C. D. (2017). Voices of aspiring teachers of color: Unraveling the double bind in teacher education. *Urban Education, 52*(8), 927–956.

Gonzalez, N. E., Moll, L., & Amanti, C. (2005). *Funds of knowledge: Theorizing practices in households, communities, and classrooms*. Lawrence Erlbaum Associates.

Grant, C. A. (1975). *Sifting and winnowing: An exploration of the relationship between Multi-cultural education and CBTE*. University of Wisconsin Teacher Corps Associate Program.

Grant, C. A. (2009). *Teach! Change! Empower!: Solutions for closing the achievement gaps*. Corwin.

Grant, C. A., & Koskela, R. A. (1986). Education that is multicultural and the relationship between preservice campus learning and field experiences. *Journal of Educational Research, 79*(4), 197–204.

Grant, C. A., & Sleeter, C. E. (2007). *Doing multicultural education for achievement and equity*. Routledge.

Graue, E. (2005). Theorizing and describing preservice teachers' images of families and schooling. *Teachers College Record, 107*(1), 157–185.

Graue, E., & Brown, C. P. (2003). Preservice teachers' notions of families and schooling. *Teaching and Teacher Education, 19*, 719–735.

Guillen, L., & Zeichner, K. (2018). A university-community partnership in teacher education from the perspectives of community-based teacher educators. *Journal of Teacher Education, 69*(2), 140–153.

Han, K. T. (2014). Moving racial discussion forward: A counterstory of racialized dynamics between an Asian–woman faculty and white preservice teachers in traditional rural America. *Journal of Diversity in Higher Education, 7*(2), 126.

Hargreaves, A., Earl, L., Moore, S., & Manning, S. (2001). *Learning to change: Teaching beyond subjects and standards*. Jossey-Bass.

hooks, b. (1994). *Teaching to transgress: Education as the practice of freedom*. Routledge.

Horton, J., & Scott, D. (2004). White students' voices in multicultural teacher education preparation. *Multicultural Education, 11*(4), 12–16.

Howard, T. (2016). *We can't teach what we don't know: White teachers, multiracial schools*. Teachers College Press.

Irizarry, J. G. (2007). Ethnic and urban intersections in the classroom: Latino students, hybrid identities, and culturally responsive pedagogy. *Multicultural Perspectives, 9*(3), 21–28.

Ishimaru, A., Bang, M., Valladares, M. R., Nolan, C. M., Tavares, H., Rajendran, A., & Chang, K. (2019). *Recasting families and communities as co-designers of education in tumultuous times*. National Education Policy Center.

Jupp, J. C., Leckie, A., Cabrera, N. L., & Utt, J. (2019). Race-evasive white teacher identity studies 1990–2015: What can we learn from 25 years of research? *Teachers College Record, 121*(1), 1–58.

Kishimoto, K. (2018). Anti-racist pedagogy: From faculty's self-reflection to organizing within and beyond the classroom. *Race Ethnicity and Education, 21*(4), 540–554.

Kohli, R. (2019). Lessons for teacher education: The role of critical professional development in teacher of color retention. *Journal of Teacher Education, 70*(1), 39–50.

Kohli, R., & Pizarro, M. (2022). The layered toll of racism in teacher education on teacher educators of color. *AERA Open, 8*.

Kumashiro, K. (2003). Against repetition: Addressing resistance to anti-oppressive change in the practices of learning, teaching, supervising, and researching. *Harvard Educational Review, 72*(1), 67–92.

Ladson-Billings, G. (1995). Toward a theory of culturally relevant pedagogy. *American Educational Research Journal, 32*(3), 465–491.

Ladson-Billings, G. (2014). Culturally relevant pedagogy 2.0: A. K. A. the remix. *Harvard Educational Review, 84*(1), 74–84.

Ladson-Billings, G. (2021). *Culturally relevant pedagogy: Asking a different question.* Teachers College Record.

Ladson-Billings, G., & Tate, W. F. (1995). Toward a critical race theory of education. *Teachers College Record, 97*(1), 47–68.

Ladson-Billings, G. J. (1999). Preparing teachers for diverse student populations: A critical race theory perspective. *Review of Research in Education, 24*, 211–247.

Ladson-Billings, G. J. (2006). From the achievement gap to the education debt: Understanding achievement in U.S. schools. *Educational Researcher, 35*(7), 3–12.

Lee, E. (1985). *Letter to Marcia: A teacher's guide to anti-racist education.* Ontario Ministry of Citizenship and Culture.

Liu, K. (2011). Enhancing prospective teachers' critical reflection in the ePortfolio environment. Ph.D. dissertation, University of Wisconsin-Madison.

Liu, K. (2015). Critical reflection as a framework for transformative learning in teacher education. *Educational Review, 67*(2), 135–157.

Liu, K. (2020). *Critical reflection for transformative learning: Understanding ePortfolios in teacher education.* Springer.

Liu, K., & Ball, A. F. (2019). Critical reflection and generativity: Toward a framework of transformative teacher education for diverse learners. *Review of Research in Education, 43*(1), 68–105.

Liu, K., Miller, R., & Ball, A. F. (2023). Teacher education for diverse learners. In R. J. Tierney, F. Rizvi, & K. Erkican (Eds.), *International encyclopedia of education, vol. 5* (pp. 356–367). Elsevier.

Liu, K., Zhang, S., Desalvo, C., & Cornejo, M. (2017). Recruit, prepare, and retain teachers of color in Nevada. *Policy Issues in Nevada Education, 2*(1), 90–108.

Lombardi, J. (2001). Supervision of student teachers: Emerging models and innovative approaches in the USA. *Teacher Development, 5*(3), 309–322.

Lopez, V., Montecinos, C., Rodriguiz, J. I., Calderon, A., & Contreras, J. F. (2012). Enacting solidarity to address peer-to-peer aggression in schools: Case studies from Chile. In C. Sleeter & E. Soriano (Eds.), *Creating solidarity across diverse communities* (pp. 23–43). Teachers College Press.

Love, B. L. (2019). *We want to do more than survive: Abolitionist teaching and the pursuit of educational freedom.* Beacon Press.

Love, B. L. (2023). *Punished for dreaming: How school reform harms Black children and how we heal.* St. Martin's Press.

Mansfield, E., & Kehoe, J. (1994). A critical examination of anti-racist education. *Canadian Journal of Education, 19*(4), 418–430.

Matias, C. E., & Mackey, J. (2016). Breakin' down whiteness in antiracist teaching: Introducing critical whiteness pedagogy. *The Urban Review, 48*, 32–50.

Maxwell, J. A. (2013). *Qualitative research design: An interactive approach* (Applied Social Science Methods Series, Vol. 41) (3rd ed.). Sage Publications.

Meier, D. (2002). *In schools we trust: Creating communities of learning in an era of testing and standardization*. Beacon.

Mezirow, J. (Ed.). (1990). *Fostering critical reflection in adulthood: A guide to transformative and emancipatory learning*. Jossey-Bass.

Miller, R., Liu, K., & Ball, A. (2020). Critical counter-narrative as transformative methodology for educational equity. *Review of Research in Education, 44*(1), 269–300.

Milner, H. R. (2003). Teacher reflection and race in cultural contexts: History, meanings, and methods in teaching. *Theory into Practice, 42*(3), 173–180.

Milner, H. R. (2006). Preservice teachers' learning about cultural and racial diversity: Implications for urban education. *Urban Education, 41*(4), 343–375.

Milner, H. R. (2007). Race, culture, and researcher positionality: Working through dangers seen, unseen, and unforeseen. *Educational Researcher, 36*(7), 388–400.

Milner, H. R. (2012). But what is urban education? *Urban Education, 47*(3), 556–561.

Milner, H. R. (2015). *Rac(e)ing to class: Confronting poverty and race in schools and classrooms*. Harvard Education Press.

Milner, H. R. (2017). Where's the race in culturally relevant pedagogy? *Teachers College Record, 119*(1), 1–32.

Milner, H. R. (2021). *Start where you are, but don't stay there: Understanding diversity, opportunity gaps, and teaching in today's classrooms*. Harvard Education Press.

Milner, H. R. (2023). *The race card: Leading the fight for truth in America's schools*. Corwin.

Milner, H. R., & Laughter, J. C. (2015). But good intentions are not enough: Preparing teachers to center race and poverty. *Urban Review, 47*(2), 341–363.

Murrell, P. C., Jr. (2000). Community teachers: A conceptual framework for preparing exemplary urban teachers. *Journal of Negro Education*, 338–348.

National Center for Education Statistics. (2023). Characteristics of Public School Teachers. *Condition of Education*. U.S. Department of Education, Institute of Education Sciences. Retrieved December 1, 2023, from https://nces.ed.gov/programs/coe/indicator/clr

Noguera, P. A. (2001). Transforming urban schools through investments in the social capital of parents. In S. Saegert, J. P. Thompson, & M. R. Warren (Eds.), *Social capital and poor communities* (pp. 189–212). Russell Sage Foundation.

Oamek, K. (2023). White preservice teachers and antiracist practice: Enabling trajectories of learning and identity in teacher preparation. *Action in Teacher Education, 46*(1), 56–74.

Paris, D. (2012). Culturally sustaining pedagogy: A needed change in stance, terminology, and practice. *Educational Researcher, 41*(3), 93–97.

Paris, D., & Alim, H. S. (Eds.). (2017). *Culturally sustaining pedagogies: Teaching and Learning for Justice in a changing world*. Teachers College Press.

Parker, L., & Hood, S. (1995). Minority students vs. majority faculty and administrators in teacher education: Perspectives on the clash of cultures. *Urban Review, 27*(2), 159–174.

Parker, L., & Lynn, M. (2002). What's race got to do with it?: Critical race theory's conflicts with and connections to qualitative research methodology and epistemology. *Qualitative Inquiry, 8*(1), 7–22.

Pettigrew, A. M. (1990). Longitudinal field Research on change: Theory and practice. *Organization Science, 1*(3), 267–292.

Picower, B. (2009). The unexamined Whiteness of teaching: How White teachers maintain and enact dominant racial ideologies. *Race Ethnicity and Education, 12*(2), 197–215.

Rodriguez-Mojica, C., Rodela, K. C., & Ott, C. (2020). "I didn't wanna believe it was a race issue": Student teaching experiences of Preservice Teachers of Color. *Urban Review, 52*, 435–457.

Sabzalian, L., Shear, S. B., & Snyder, J. (2021). Standardizing Indigenous erasure: A TribalCrit and QuantCrit analysis of K-12 US civics and government standards. *Theory & Research in Social Education, 47*(3), 321–359.

Saldaña, J. (2003). *Longitudinal qualitative research: Analyzing change through time*. Altamira.

Saldana, J. (2013). *The coding manual for qualitative researchers* (2nd ed.).

Schon, D. A. (1983). *The reflective practitioner: How professionals think in action*. Basic Books.

Sleeter, C., & Thao, Y. (2007). Guest editors' introduction: Diversifying the teaching force. *Teacher Education Quarterly, 34*(4), 3–8.

Sleeter, C. E. (2001). Preparing teachers for culturally diverse schools: Research and the overwhelming presence of Whiteness. *Journal of Teacher Education, 52*, 94–106.

Sleeter, C. E. (2017). Critical race theory and the whiteness of teacher education. *Urban Education, 52*(2), 155–169.

Sundstrom, R. R. (2003). Review: Arrogance, love, and identity in the American struggle with race. *Social Theory and Practice, 29*(1), 159–172.

Swann Report. (1985). *Education for all: Report of the committee of enquiry into the education of children from ethnic minority groups*. Her Majesty's Stationery Office.

Taylor, D. E. (2016). *The rise of the American conservation movement: Power, privilege, and environmental protection*. Duke University Press.

Valenzuela, C. A. (2017). Sonic borderland literacies: A re/mix of culturally relevant education. *Journal of Pedagogy, Pluralism, and Practice, 9*(1), 33.

Villegas, A. M., & Davis, D. E. (2008). Preparing teachers of color to confront racial/ethnic disparities in educational outcomes. In *Handbook of research on teacher education* (pp. 583–605). Routledge.

Villegas, A. M., & Irvine, J. J. (2010). Diversifying the teaching force: An examination of major arguments. *Urban Review, 42*(3), 175–192.

Villegas, A. M., Strom, K., & Lucas, T. (2012). Closing the racial/ethnic gap between students of color and their teachers: An elusive goal. *Equity & Excellence in Education, 45*(2), 283–301.

Washington, V. (1981). Impact of antiracism/multicultural education training on elementary teachers' attitudes and classroom behavior. *Elementary School Journal, 81*(3), 186–192.

Watson, J. K. P. (1988). From assimilation to anti-racism: Changing educational policies in England and Wales. *Journal of Multilingual and Multicultural Development, 9*(6), 531–552.

Welch, K., Lehmann, P. S., Chouhy, C., & Chiricos, T. (2022). Cumulative racial and ethnic disparities along the school-to-prison pipeline. *Journal of Research in Crime and Delinquency, 59*(5), 574–626.

Woodson, A., & Pabon, A. (2016). "I'm none of the above:" Exploring themes of heteropatriarchy in the life histories of Black male educators. *Equity & Excellence in Education, 47*(1), 57–71.

Yosso, T. J. (2005). Whose culture has capital? A critical race theory discussion of community cultural wealth. *Race Ethnicity and Education, 8*(1), 69–91.

Yosso, T. J. (2006). *Critical race counterstories along the Chicana/Chicano educational pipeline.* Routledge.

Zeichner, K., Bowman, M., Guillen, L., & Napolitan, K. (2016). Engaging and working in solidarity with local communities in preparing the teachers of their children. *Journal of Teacher Education, 67*(4), 277–290.

Zeichner, K. M., & Liston, D. P. (1996). *Reflective teaching: An introduction.* Erlbaum.

Zygmunt, E., Cipollone, K., Clark, P., & Tancock, S. (2018a). Community-engaged teacher preparation. In *Oxford research encyclopedia of education.* Oxford University Press.

Zygmunt, E., Cipollone, K., Tancock, S., Clausen, J., Clark, P., & Mucherah, W. (2018b). Loving out loud: Community mentors, teacher candidates, and transformational learning through a pedagogy of care and connection. *Journal of Teacher Education, 69*(2), 127–139.

CHAPTER 3

From Camouflage to Pledging Commitment: Race in the Habits of Mind

As we discussed in Chap. 1, *habits of mind* are "habitual ways of thinking, feeling and acting influenced by assumptions that constitute a set of codes … that may be cultural, social, educational, economic, political, or psychological" (Mezirow, 1997, p. 7). Habits of mind may be deliberately inculcated through formal learning processes, but more commonly they constitute a kind of unconsidered "habitus" (Bourdieu, 1977) adopted through socialization from childhood to early adulthood. Therefore, habits of mind are susceptible to critical reflection, starting from the very first step of assumption analysis before any transformative actions occur (Liu, 2015). However, when left unchallenged, they tend to reproduce unconsidered assumptions grounded in broad social and political practices, including race, ethnicity, class, gender, religion, sexual orientation, ability, etc. Our analysis of prospective teachers' written reflections and interviews reveals their habits of mind regarding race and racism through <u>four</u> general approaches which we detail in the rest of this chapter.

1. They *camouflaged* their discussion of race and racism with either silence or with the use of euphemisms such as "diversity" and "culture."
2. They *simplified* deep structural practices of racism into issues of trust and personal behavior.

K. Liu et al., *Preparing White Teachers for Anti-Racist Education*, https://doi.org/10.1007/978-3-031-73534-9_3

3. They *held deficit views toward minoritized students and* engaged in *criminalizing their behaviors.*
4. They *pledged commitment* to fighting injustice at some unspecified point in the future and depicted themselves as *saviors* of minoritized students.

3.1   CAMOUFLAGING

Prospective teachers rarely talked about race or racial issues in their written reflections. When they did, they tended to avoid the terms "race" and "racism," using deracializing language (Yoon, 2012) such as "culture," "diversity," and "families." These habits of mind echo what other researchers have found that prospective teachers tend to use safer terms such as culture to replace race (Ladson-Billings, 2009; Milner, 2009). For example, Judy reflected at the beginning of her third semester practicum that she was a "minority" in her classroom.

> I was nervous at first because I was entering a classroom which consisted of mainly African American, Latino, Asian, and Indian students. There are no Caucasian students. I wasn't quite sure what to expect, and I was nervous because I would be the minority. (Judy ePortfolio Reflection)

Judy's initial reaction was to state a desire to learn about her students, but the way in which she phrased that goal was without reference to students' racial and ethnic backgrounds although clearly she reflected earlier that the students in the classroom were mainly African American, Latin[x], and Asian:

> Because I felt this anxiety of stepping into a very different classroom than I had ever experienced, I created a goal to learn as much about these students as I possibly could and then incorporate their interests, hobbies and experiences into my teaching. (Judy ePortfolio Reflection)

Judy did not mention race in any way in the rest of her ePortfolio reflections for her third, fourth, and fifth semesters despite the fact that, based on our observations, her classroom each semester had students from racially diverse backgrounds. Instead, she mentioned multiple times that she strove to implement culturally responsive teaching. For example, in her final thoughts at the end of her student teaching semester, Judy reflected,

I would like to stretch myself further and extend my teaching towards a culturally responsive manner. As I continue to work on building community experiences with students, families and other community members organically in my life, I will learn more about students' lives and the communities they live in. (Judy ePortfolio Reflection)

In short, what appears to begin as a reflection on race became one about students' hobbies, lives, families, and communities.

Similarly, Ella (Midwestern University) was very vocal about diversity and equity in her ePortfolio. However, when talking about her own students in the classroom, she never mentioned the students' racial backgrounds, but focused on language and culture. For example

My art/math computer game had the shapes translated into each language that is represented in my classroom. The students lit up when they recognized the language as something they hear at home. Additionally, one of my student's parents did the translation and he was thrilled when he realized that it was his dad. Having the students feel that their culture is important in the classroom was important to me. (Ella ePortfolio Reflection)

A different sort of camouflaging occurs when prospective teachers retreat into statistics or abstractions rather than thinking in terms of the students in their classroom. For example, throughout the whole ePortfolio reflection, Karla never talked about the racial backgrounds of her students. When asked about the demographics of her students during her student teaching semester, Karla responded:

Well, I believe there are 37% for reduced lunch, that's the real statistic I found. I know my classroom is not very diverse at all. It's majority of White students. But then the other two 4th and 5th grade students do have higher African American populations. There's a couple of Indians, like Southeast Asian students. I don't know if there's any Hispanic. I didn't notice it. The reason I don't know is because it's a new school, I don't think all the demographics are online or available. (Karla interview)

Similar patterns were observed from the other prospective teachers' ePortfolio reflections. For example, Cathy (Clear Water University) reflected:

This past week, I focused on Standard 10, in which I employed varied instructional strategies into my teaching. To do this, it helped me focus on the skill of "how to teach" in a classroom full of diverse people and diverse learners. (Cathy ePortfolio Reflection)

Helen (Desert View University) reflected that

This site has given me the opportunity to work with children who are considered "at risk" youth. This means that these children do not have the resources that many other children do, such as parents to help with homework, or a consistent supply of food on the table. (Helen Reflection)

3.2   SIMPLIFYING

White prospective teachers' habit of camouflaging diversity as culture brings us to the second finding, simplifying: They made *simple generalizations* about the connection between race, culture, and behavior, or collapsed racial politics into personal integrity issues. Judy provides a very clear example. Her ePortfolio never discussed Olivia, the sole African American student in her student teaching classroom. During the interviews, however, Judy discussed Olivia at some length because she presented, in Judy's view, a behavior problem. She first described Olivia as:

really very different from the rest of the kids in our class. She is the only African American in our class. For the first month or month and half, there was a huge like just divide in our class. It took a long time for the kids to kind of accept her because she was just different, because she's from a totally different cultural group and upbringing. (Judy Interview)

Judy went on to describe Olivia's unfamiliarity with the basics of school routine and authority structures, and considered that these routines might not be "equitable" for all students. However, the basis for her critique was that students don't all share the same "culture," missing the crucial point that classroom routines assume prior knowledge of formal schooling that is constructed on the basis of the White norm. She simplified the problem as stemming from Olivia's culture, not from the school's: "I think that's her culture. So she feels like she can move her body 'cause she wants to move her body" (Judy Interview).

Karla, as mentioned above, did not mention race in her written reflections. In her journal entry for the week in which she was required to demonstrate her ability to "employ varied instructional strategies," she used phrases such as "diverse," "ethnicity," and "culture"; however, there are no details linking this statement to her students:

> In a classroom full of diverse people and diverse learners, it is crucial to vary the strategies used to instruct those children. Students are not only on multiple cognitive and emotional levels, but they also come from a wide background of ethnicity and culture. (Karla, ePortfolio Reflection)

Ella demonstrated a more sophisticated kind of simplification: She overstated the role of "representation" as a purpose of racial equity, such as summing up the lesson she learned from a classroom activity in which she invited parents to read different shapes in their home language. Ella explained her motivation for this activity was that "students need to see themselves in the classroom," but then asked "if students were taught by teachers of their race, would we be reinstating segregation?" (Ella ePortfolio). The latter statement did not mention or critique the reality that most students in the district where she was placed were taught by White teachers. Both statements minimize institutional racism, the first by restricting the problem to identity matching, and the second by naturalizing the Whiteness of the current teacher corps, making diversity in the teacher corps a problematic state.

Simplification also occurred in reflections describing interactions with African American students, White prospective teachers praising themselves for earning Black students' acceptance and respect as evidence of "race is not an issue." According to Abby (Clear Water University),

> I grew up in a rural city that was predominantly White. At the elementary school I am placed now, 80% of the students in after school clubs were Black and 75% came from low-income families. I didn't know how to act around the kids because I looked different .... At first the kids pointed out my differences. Some of the boys called me "White girl" and one of the girls told me she didn't like my blond hair. After a couple of days the kids started to get to know me and become very accepting of my personality. Many of the kids that teased me in the beginning became the kids that I spent the most time with. (Abby ePortfolio Reflection)

She continued to reflect on how she felt about this success: "I felt great about this because they took my suggestions and used them. They realized that I was not an enemy, and that they could accept me as a contributor to this race topic." (Abby ePortfolio Reflection)

Cathy reflected similarly that when she first was placed in a classroom with a few African American students, an African American boy told her that his father told him that White people cannot be trusted. Instead of understanding this statement from a historical perspective, she defended herself by saying she could be trusted. She further reflected that the boy finally accepted who she was:

> One boy told me that he wanted to paint me Black so that I would fit in better. I asked him where he heard that and why he felt that way. I told him that I can't change who I am, and he proceeded to tell me that his father had told him that all White people couldn't be trusted. We had an extensive conversation about why this wasn't the case, and why I AM able to be trusted. But, this experience goes to show that there are many complexities that go along with the issue of race, and it is with the children presently that this issue is going to be solved in the future. This boy has grown to really like being around me, and I think he has since been able to look beyond my skin color and be able to accept me for who I am. (Cathy, ePortfolio Reflection)

Note the simplification of difference into appearance, as well as the slippage of racial issues into one of Cathy being "accepted" as trustworthy by a Black student. Similarly, Abby reflected that "the girls would sit and brush my blonde hair and I would play with the strings of beads around their braids. Outside, I learned to 'double dutch' and we all played football together" (Abby, ePortfolio Reflection). Both of these reflections suggest a need for the White preservice teachers to demonstrate their removal from the racial structures and practices of US school and society, to be able to assert that they were not racist.

Here, Cathy and Abby used mutual affection and physical proximity to demonstrate their closeness to students of another race—but had the effect of masking the depth and complexity of racism existing in our society. From a CRT lens, this simplification is highly problematic, eliding the power relations (racial, gender-based, age-based, and institutional) that mediated both the children's initial response to the teacher and their "transformation." Moreover, there is a particularly troubling note in Cathy's report of an "extensive conversation" regarding why the father's assertion that "all White people can't be trusted" "wasn't the case." She didn't indicate how that conversation proceeded, whether the child engaged in back-and-forth or simply remained silent. Nevertheless, Cathy believed that she successfully convinced the child that what his father said was not true. Such agreement from the side of the Black student can be a sign of *micro-coercion* and *micro-control* (Edwards et al., 2022), a form of micro-aggression experienced by individuals on the weak side of a power differential—such as a child when contradicted by their teacher. During an episode of micro-coercion, the person subjected to the coercion chooses not to respond rather than risk the consequences of escalating a micro-aggression; they are coerced into appearing to agree in order to speed an end to the episode. From this standpoint, rather than demonstrating Cathy's freedom from racism, her effort to control the student's understanding of race relations by denying his father's position simply reinforced the idea that White people have the power to control how they are perceived by minoritized communities. Finally, by negating the father's position—and thereby denying his life experiences as a Black man in the United States—Cathy also denied the intergenerational experiences of racial trauma.

3.3   Deficit Views and Criminalizing

Our analysis demonstrates that White prospective teachers held deficit views toward minoritized students by using behaviors and performances of White students as the norm (Milner, 2023) and tended to criminalize behaviors by minoritized students that they ignored or explained away when seen in White children. Some of the White participants articulated their assumptions about their minoritized students by using phrases such as "struggling," "problematic," and "hard to teach." Helen (Desert View University) used the linkage of poverty and laziness to describe minoritized students and their families stating that

> All students have equal opportunities. If you work hard, you can be successful. If you fail, you have to rethink what the reasons are. It is true that some students are from poor families and they struggle. But that should not be an excuse and if you don't work hard and are being lazy, nobody can help you. (Helen, Class Discussion)

Some White prospective teachers described minoritized students as "defiant," "aggressive," "dangerous" and thus needing to be "controlled." In an interview, Craig (Desert View University) described an African American boy as very aggressive and defiant. When he has a conflict with another student, we need to immediately have him under control. Otherwise, he can be dangerous to the other students. A gentle reminder would not work for him and we should not put other students in danger. (Craig Interview)

As described earlier, Judy assumed Olivia, an African American girl, was "difficult" and "defiant." Instead of embracing Olivia's desire to be in control of her learning as evidence of independence and leadership skills, she treated it as a "defiance," attributed it to "her culture," and marked it as behavior that needed to be controlled. Judy described Olivia as

very challenging. You know, she's very defiant, very much "I am in control, this is how I am going to do things," and you know .... I think that's her culture ... So what we are doing is we give her one chance and then if she did it again, or didn't listen, or talk back, she was out. But I think she needed that; she needed the consequence; otherwise she would walk over you. (Judy Interview)

Abby (Clear Water University) also demonstrated a deficit view of minoritized students and criminalized their behaviors in her student teaching classroom. Abby conducted her student teaching in a predominantly White first grade classroom in the small Midwestern town where the university is located. One student, Jamal, is Black. According to Abby, Jamal's parents were from Niger and Jamal was born in Chicago; his parents went back to Niger when he was little and they had just returned to the United States at the start of the school year. When Jamal joined the first grade classroom, he did not have prior schooling experience in the United States. During the first few class observations, we noticed that Jamal's name was constantly being called: "Jamal, eyes on the board .... Jamal, keep your hands to yourself ... Jamal, sit up still." In one observation, it was counted Jamal's name being called five times in ten minutes for discipline purposes such as "Jamal, eyes on here" and "Jamal, are your eyes on the board?" It was obvious that these in-classroom disciplines were primarily focusing on Jamal's behaviors and made him hyper-visible in a criminalizing way, showing little care to guide Jamal's academic work. In an interview with Abby and her mentor teacher, Katrina asked what they thought of Jamal. Both Abby and her mentor teacher provided a detailed, deficit-based description of what Jamal was lacking:

Abby: He is pretty fluent in English but he doesn't know phrases. He doesn't do well in tests probably because he doesn't know the directions.

Mentor Teacher: He does not want to do his work.

Abby: Yah yah, he always wants the other people to work for him. He won't read, he doesn't like to read, unless you read with him.

Mentor Teacher: I think because he is the younger one in his family, his sister always does things for him.

Katrina: I noticed that his name was called a lot.

Abby: Yes he needs that. It helps him to concentrate.

Mentor Teacher: You should have watched him at the beginning of the semester. He would run out of the class and run to the hallway. We had to literally block him at the door. He is getting much better now.

Abby: Yes, exactly! We had to literally grab his arms.

From this conversation, it is obvious that both Abby and her mentor teacher assumed that Jamal did not want to work independently because of his family structure. Also, without considering the reality that Jamal needed some time to learn and become accustomed to the classroom routines, they used criminalizing and dehumanizing approaches to control and punish his body such as blocking him at the door and grabbing his arms. Similar to Judy's habits of mind toward Olivia, Abby and her mentor teacher also assumed that these dehumanizing discipline approaches were necessary to save Jamal from causing further troubles.

Clearly these deficit-based assumptions mirror the larger controlling narratives; they were not grounded in truth but reflected the racial grammar that frames dominant and hegemonic perceptions as truth against minoritized students and families (Bonilla-Silva, 2012). This dominant racial grammar of deficit further justify the dehumanizing and criminalizing approaches exerted on them. These findings indicate that the deficit thinking and criminalizing of minoritized students by White prospective teachers at times occasioned professions of purity on the part of the participants, framed either as a pledge to commit to social justice and equity or through a "White savior complex" (Emdin, 2016) that we are turn to in the next section.

3.4   Pledging Commitment and Savior Making

White prospective teachers sometimes acknowledged the social reality of inequity outside their classroom, pledging commitment to equity and social justice. In her third semester reflection, for example, Ella proclaimed,

> I will bring outside information into the classroom (ie) nature, demographics, social justice, in order to make math more meaningful to the students. This will involve parent and community interaction and will encourage the students to make real connections with the curriculum. (Ella ePortfolio Reflection)

Similarly, Judy stated during the student teaching semester that achieving equity was her goal: "The principle of equity is what I strive to achieve in and out of my classroom. For me, it is the common thread in my thinking about students, planning, and reflection" (Judy ePortfolio Reflection). Although Karla never pledged commitment to equity and social justice in her ePortfolio, she did state multiple times her commitment to connect curriculum to her students, the community, and the larger social context:

> Part of my role as a teacher is to connect the curriculum and student learning to the social context in which their schooling occurs. As my education philosophy states, I value the importance of community and other factors as part of the learning process for my students. (Karla ePortfolio Reflection)

Pledging commitment was common in other participants' written reflections and interviews. For example, Cathy stated in her ePortfolio reflection that

> I strongly believe that diversity should be incorporated into every lesson or activity. I would use the Transformation Approach, where the structure of the curriculum is changed to allow students to view concepts and themes from the perspectives of diverse ethnic and cultural groups. (Cathy ePortfolio Reflection)

Similarly, Craig (Desert View University) reflected that "I would strive to support all the students in my classroom. My job as a teacher is to ensure all students are treated equally and have the opportunities to achieve their greatest potential." Helen (Desert View University) reflected that if the student needs extra support in learning because of cultural dif-ference, I will come up with as many strategies as I can to help them understand. By having an open mind and open heart, I believe you can provide your students with anything they need and provide them with opportunities to succeed. (Helen reflection)

Prospective teachers often followed their pledging with evidence of success in working with minoritized students, depicting the students with a deficit view (Milner, 2008) and a culture of poverty (Ladson-Billings, 2006b) that Valencia (2010) theorizes as a process of seeing difference in pathological terms and assuming the position of savior. They sometimes held up themselves as a model to be emulated by minoritized children so that they could be "successful," praising themselves for how good they were at improving the lives of children of color. In other words, White prospective teachers saw themselves as *saviors* of children of color through their ability to improve their academic performance and future life poten-tial. For example, Cathy (Clear Water University) reflected that

The students in my class have proved that I can work with children of a different race so well by approaching them as real people with a sincere desire to improve their situation academically. Improving their academic performance will help them achieve success in life ....For example, I was able to teach one of the children how to multiply for the first time, which was a huge step for this particular child. There had been many people in the placement who had tried to teach multiplication to this child without success, but I was able to have success. I did this by showing this child that I was a friend and not a teacher or an enemy. This child learned to trust me, and this made an avenue for me to teach him how to multiply. Through this understanding of each other, and a little humor, I was able to reach this child in a way that nobody else at the placement was able to. (Cathy ePortfolio Reflection)

Note the multiple themes at play in this extended reflection from Cathy: savior-making, earning trust, mentioning race only in the abstract. The self-praise is particularly striking, founded as it is on being "a friend and not a teacher or an enemy." This is a somewhat more elaborate way for the prospective teacher to declare "I am not a racist." It reflects the "color blindness" or "color evasiveness" underlying the denial of White privilege common among prospective teachers (Annamma et al., 2016; Choi, 2008).

Savior-making was also visible as the subtext of pledging commitment, as in Judy's statement that, "as an educator, I will continue to fight for the equality for all citizens and stick to the principle of justice" (Judy ePortfolio). Such statements proclaim a remarkable reservoir of strength and privilege to expend in a mission of truth and justice that is the well from which savior-making is drawn, and suggests greater interest in self-satisfaction than results. Similarly, savior-making underlies some of the celebratory statements of the prospective teacher's success in the classroom that might go unremarked in other circumstances. For example, at one point in her description of a classroom activity she deliberately engineered to be inclusive (described in more detail below), Ella remarked, "The ability to affirm these students' identities was so fulfilling ... *Having the students feel that their culture is important in the classroom was important to me*" (Ella ePortfolio, emphasis by the authors). From the surface level, this statement might seem quite positive—yes, it is important that students' home cultures be valued in the classroom. CRT, however, forces us to ask *for whom* is it important? The answer here—for the prospective teacher herself—is a troubling reminder of what drives savior-making. It is the need to feel the satisfaction of being the savior above the needs of the students of color being "saved."

On a different occasion, Helen (Desert View University), who equated "poverty" with "struggle" and "laziness" in her description of her placement in low-income neighborhood schools, explicitly took on a savior role, saying,

> A huge thing I had to remember was that I was working in a place where some students who didn't know they were different from others and I wanted to make sure that blissful feeling continued on with them through life. (Helen, Reflection)

Helen's ability to "save" minoritized students, leveraged as it was on her assumption of their ignorance of (her beliefs about) their lives, demonstrated a deficit view of her students, assuming their being different is a threat for their identity development. It further demonstrated Helen's evasion of race and refusal to learn about the lives, strengths, and assets of these students and their families that can contribute to their own education and the education of others. For Helen, the way to save these students is to cover their eyes as she had covered her own, shielding them from being aware of their real identities.

3.5   Challenging the Habits of Minds

Prospective teachers' habits of mind revealed above show that teacher education has an important role to play in dealing with complex issues prospective teachers face in the process of learning to be anti-racist teachers. These habits of mind, on the one hand, are not surprising because they are representative of long taken-for-granted assumptions about people of color (Milner, 2008). On the other hand, race continues to be a key problem in our society; institutional racism, in particular, has proven difficult to address piecemeal.

We found that prospective teachers use generic terms such as "culture" and "cultural diversity" to camouflage race and racial issues without considering the details of the learners, nor the nature of the (White) norms from which they diverge. This imprecision might stem from a lack of clarity in teacher education programs themselves—a "conceptual confusion" (Grant et al., 2004, p. 200). As Pollock et al. (2010) observed, teacher educators are quick to use the term *diversity*, but "they share no unified definition of what an educator prepared for diversity actually looks like, how such an educator should get prepared, or how his or her preparation could best be assessed" (p. 212).

Prospective teachers' habits of mind also confirm serious concerns raised by Gutiérrez and Rogoff (2003), González (2005), Ladson-Billings (2009), Milner (2010, 2014, 2017), Howard (2013), and others that the overuse of "cultural" diversity, and especially the way in which it replaced race at the center of multicultural education, means that culture has "lost much of its utility as a way to describe the diversity within society" (González, 2005, p. 36). Prospective teachers' approach of making simple generalizations about the connection between race, culture, and behavior speaks well to the problem of lack of emphasis on analyzing how racism operates in the classroom (Ladson-Billings, 2006a). For example, when Abby reflected on how a student wanted to "paint me Black so that I would fit in better," Abby treated it simply as a lack of trust from the student without reflecting further on the social and historical factors that might have impacted the student's understanding of racial differences. According Winans (2010), children's assertions may "reveal important insights on how their educational experiences (both inside and outside the classroom) may have contributed to the formation of a belief system around racial difference in which "racialized" interpretations and assessments of individuals can be made" (p. 76). To support prospective teachers to understand racial socialization—"the transmission from adults to children of information regarding race" (Hughes et al., 2006, p. 748)—teacher educators need to provide prospective teachers with racial literacy to critically examine and analyze "how race and racism inform beliefs, interpretive frameworks, practices, cultures, and institutions" (Winans, 2010, p. 477).

White prospective teachers in this study demonstrated a deficit view of minoritized students, pathologizing and criminalizing them and their families by using terms such as "aggressive," "defiant," and "struggling." They often insisted that they needed to be punished and controlled. Their punishment and controlling were justified by prospective teachers as they were "good" for the ones being controlled. Punishment saved them from getting into bigger trouble, and more importantly, protected the "safety" of their White peers. These findings are in line with previous research (Annamma et al., 2019; Basile et al., 2019; Bryan, 2017) that revealed students of color are often dehumanized and are perceived to be dangerous. Our findings also demonstrate challenges teacher education programs face in dislodging White supremacist perceptions among prospective teachers.

The habits of mind of prospective teachers regarding race and racism indicate that we have much work to do in teacher education. Without seriously addressing the racism and inequity in education and society, these habits of mind will continue unabated, replicating many problems in schools and society. Gusa (2010) points out that,

> unexamined historically situated White cultural ideology embedded in the language, cultural practices, traditions, and perceptions of knowledge, allow these institutions to remain racialized. (p. 465)

Gusa continues to observe that White normative messages and practices "remain subtle, nebulous, and unnamed, they potentially harm the well-being, self-esteem, and academic success of those who do not share the norms of the White culture" (p. 471). Gusa's observation is certainly evident in our results. The key to addressing institutional racism with prospective teachers lies in developing their capacity for critical reflection in service to transformative learning with particular attention to race and racism in daily practice. It is not enough to provide general courses—mostly through the one-shot solution (Zeichner, 1993)—on race, ethnicity, and multicultural education, expecting prospective teachers to extrapolate to their own lived practice. Rather, prospective teachers must be supported to analyze fundamental race-based habits of mind in their daily practice and the larger society through all the coursework and field experiences in their teacher education program, reflecting critically on those assumptions to springboard their own transformative actions in their teaching (Liu & Ball, 2019). CRT is therefore vital not just for analyzing prospective teachers' thoughts and actions but also for helping them recognize habits of mind and patterns of acting that reinforce racism in their classrooms.

The problem, then, is not just one for prospective teachers but also for teacher educators: Our analysis of prospective teachers' habits of mind reveals that they were able to pledge commitment to social justice and equity in their written reflections. Liu (2020) revealed that one reason they did so was that they were *expected* to demonstrate their commitment to social justice and equity in written reflections that were evaluated for licensure purposes. In an evaluative environment where they were expected to articulate how they met the standards and prove they were equity-oriented teachers, prospective teachers tended to reflect on their successes in working with students of color. As teacher educators, should we stop here and be satisfied with their pledges and their stories of success based on their written reflection and self-selected evidence? Instead, we argue that we need to explore further to discern the patterns of acting. How do they carry out their teaching practice, especially in teaching and supporting minoritized students on a daily basis? It is to the second part of this question we turn in Chap. 4.

REFERENCES

Annamma, S. A., Anyon, Y., Joseph, N., Farrar, J., Greer, E., Downing, B., & Simmons, J. (2019). Black girls and school discipline: The complexities of being overrepresented and understudied. *Urban Education, 54*(2), 211–242.

Annamma, S. A., Jackson, D. D., & Morrison, D. (2016). Conceptualizing color-evasiveness: Using dis/ability critical race theory to expand a color-blind racial ideology in education and society. *Race Ethnicity and Education, 20*(2), 147–162.

Basile, V., York, A., & Black, R. (2019). Who's the one being disrespectful? Understanding and deconstructing the criminalization of elementary school boys of color. *Urban Education, 57*(9), 1592–1620.

Bonilla-Silva, E. (2012). The invisible weight of whiteness: The racial grammar of everyday life in America. *Michigan Sociological Review, 26*(1), 1–15.

Bourdieu, P. (1977). *Outline of a theory of practice.* Cambridge University Press.

Bryan, N. (2017). White teachers' role in sustaining the school-to-prison pipeline: Recommendations for teacher education. *Urban Review, 49*, 326–345.

Choi, J. (2008). *Unlearning colorblind ideologies in education class* (pp. 53–71). *Educational Foundations.*

Edwards, M., Mitchell, L., Abe, C., Cooper, E., Johansson, J., & Ridgway, M. (2022). "I am not a gentleman ccademic:" Telling our truths of micro-coercive control and gaslighting in business schools using "faction". *Gender, Work & Organization*, 1–20.

Emdin, C. (2016). *For White folks who teach in the hood... and the rest of y'all Too: Reality pedagogy and urban education.* Beacon Press.

González, N. (2005). Beyond culture: The hybridity of funds of knowledge. In N. González, L. Moll, & C. Amanti (Eds.), *Funds of knowledge: Theorizing practices in households, communities, and classrooms.* Routledge.

Grant, C. A., Elsbree, A. R., & Fondrie, S. (2004). A decade of research on the changing terrain of multicultural education research. In J. A. Banks & C. A. M. G. Banks (Eds.), *Handbook of research on multicultural education* (2nd ed., pp. 184–207). Jossey-Bass.

Gusa, D. L. (2010). White institutional presence: The impact of whiteness on campus climate. *Harvard Educational Review, 80*(4), 464–490.

Gutiérrez, K., & Rogoff, B. (2003). Cultural ways of learning: Individual traits or repertoires of practice. *Educational Researcher, 32*(5), 19–25.

Howard, T. C. (2013). How does it feel to be a problem? Black male students, schools, and learning in enhancing the knowledge base to disrupt deficit frameworks. *Review of Research in Education, 37*(1), 54–86.

Hughes, D., Smith, E. P., Stevenson, H. C., Rodriquez, J., Johnson, D. J., & Spicer, P. (2006). Parents' ethnic-racial socialization practices: A review of research and directions for future study. *Developmental Psychology, 42*(5), 747–770.

Ladson-Billings, G. (2006a). They're trying to wash us away: The adolescence of critical race theory in education. In A. D. Dixson & C. K. Rousseau (Eds.), *Critical race theory in education: All God's children got a song* (pp. v–xiii). Routledge.

Ladson-Billings, G. (2006b). It's not the culture of poverty, it's the poverty of culture: The problem with Teacher Education. *Anthropology and Education Quarterly, 37*(2), 104.

Ladson-Billings, G. (2009). Just what is critical race theory and what's it doing in a nice field like education? In E. Taylor, D. Gillborn, & G. Ladson-Billings (Eds.), *Foundations of critical race theory in education* (pp. 17–36). Routledge.

Liu, K. (2015). Critical reflection as a framework for transformative learning in teacher education. *Educational Review, 67*(2), 135–157.

Liu, K. (2020). *Critical reflection for transformative learning: Understanding ePortfolios in teacher education.* Springer.

Liu, K., & Ball, A. (2019). Critical reflection and generativity: Toward a framework of transformative teacher education for diverse learners. *Review of Research in Education, 43*(1), 68–105.

Mezirow, J. (1997). Transformative learning: Theory to practice. In P. Cranton (Ed.), *Transformative learning in action: Insights from practice (New Directions for Adult and Continuing Education)* (pp. 5–12). Jossey-Bass.

Milner, H. R. (2008). Disrupting deficit notions of differences: Counter-narratives of teachers and community in urban education. *Teaching and Teacher Education, 24*(6), 1573–1589.

Milner, H. R. (2009). African-American males in urban schools: No excuses – Teach and empower. In H. R. Milner (Ed.), *Diversity and education: Teachers, teaching, and teacher education* (pp. 5–16). Charles C. Thomas.

Milner, H. R. (2010). What does teacher education have to do with teaching? Implications for diversity studies. *Journal of Teacher Education, 61*(1–2), 118–131.

Milner, H. R. (2014). Teacher education and Black communities: Implications for equity, access, and achievement. In C. W. Lewis, Y. Sealy-Ruiz, & I. Toldson (Eds.), *Teacher education and Black communities: Implications for access, equity, and achievement* (pp. 317–321). Information Age Publishing.

Milner, H. R. (2017). Where's the race in culturally relevant pedagogy? *Teachers College Record, 119*(1), 1–32.

Milner, H. R. (2023). *The race card: Leading the fight for truth in America's schools*. Corwin.

Pollock, M., Deckman, S., & Mira, M. C. (2010). 'But what can I do?' Three necessary tensions in teaching teachers about race. *Journal of Teacher Education, 61*(3), 211–224.

Valencia, R. R. (2010). *Dismantling contemporary deficit thinking: Educational thought and practice*. Routledge.

Winans, A. E. (2010). Cultivating racial literacy in White, segregated settings: Emotions as sites of ethical engagement. *Curriculum Inquiry, 40*(3), 475–491.

Yoon, I. H. (2012). The paradoxical nature of whiteness-at-work in the daily life of schools and teacher communities. *Race Ethnicity and Education, 15*(5), 587–613.

Zeichner, K. (1993). Traditions of practice in U.S. preservice teacher education programs. *Teaching and Teacher Education, 9*(1), 1–13.

CHAPTER 4

One Step Forward, Two Steps Back: Racism in the Patterns of Acting

In Chap. 3, we focused on unpacking White prospective teachers' habits of mind regarding race and racism. We found that they tended to *camouflage*, speaking around race using terms such as "difference" or "diversity." They also tended to *simplify* race and racism to terms such as "culture" (left undefined) or construct cross-race relationships solely in terms of personal affect, elided history, and power relations. They also tended to hold deficit views toward minoritized students and criminalize their behaviors. White preservice teachers also leaned toward *pledging commitment* to educational equity and position themselves as *saviors* of their minoritized students.

From Mezirow's (1990) point of view, habits of mind are not just an issue of viewpoint affecting how individuals understand and interpret the world, but also direct how they act in society. Therefore, in the context of this study, after gaining knowledge about White prospective teachers' habits of mind regarding race and racism, our job as teachers educators was not over. We needed to further make sense of how they actually dealt with race and racism in their teaching—their patterns of acting, and more importantly, based on this understanding to support them to critically analyze their assumptions that can lead to transformative actions in their practice. Therefore, we conducted intensive classroom observations of each of the participants to document their patterns of acting on a daily basis.

© The Author(s), under exclusive license to Springer Nature Switzerland AG 2024
K. Liu et al., *Preparing White Teachers for Anti-Racist Education*,
https://doi.org/10.1007/978-3-031-73534-9_4

All the three teacher education programs where the White prospective teachers in this study learned to teach required them to demonstrate ability to teach and support all the students in their classrooms. The demonstration was primarily done through lesson plans, directly observed and/or recorded lessons by supervisors, and written reflections. As discussed in Chap. 3, all seven White prospective teachers pledged commitment to teach for social justice and equity. In their real classroom action, they made efforts to perform in accord with their pledge in prepared lessons, especially the ones being observed by their supervisors. Judy and Ella enacted a unit specifically focusing on equity; the other five participants designed some activities to conduct culturally relevant teaching based on their own understanding of what this meant. However, in unscripted situations, when confronted with racism in the classroom, the prospective teachers' pledged commitment was not sustained. Instead, closely tracking their deficit-based and criminalizing habits of mind, they backslid, returning to a pattern of inequitable treatment of minoritized students through actions such as policing, interrogating, public shaming, and segregating the students. Even in the context of a prepared lesson, racism in the form of subconscious institutional reinforcement upended the plans, breaking through the careful demonstration of equity to expose the race-based nature of the classroom experience.

4.1   PERFORMING IN PREPARED LESSONS

During Judy's student teaching, she designed a unit specifically to focus on equity. Since the unit would fall during the holiday season toward the end of the fall semester, Judy wrote in her ePortfolio that she wanted her students to have "an opportunity to learn about lesser known celebrations" (Judy ePortfolio). Therefore, she invited community members to introduce the celebrations from their own cultures. This included inviting an African American teacher to demonstrate Kwanzaa and a Jewish parent to show Hanukkah. After the unit, Judy reflected that her students learned the principles of different celebrations of light: "We made Kwanzaa mats and cups. We learned about the 7 principles and applied the principles to our own lives" (Judy ePortfolio).

Ella made an effort to make use of her students' cultural backgrounds to support her teaching. In her unit on geometric shapes, she made a computer game for her students to learn different geometric shapes and invited her students' parents to read the shapes in their home language and recorded them doing so. When students clicked a shape, the computer spoke the name of the shape with the voice and language of a parent. Ella reflected the process and her rationale for this strategy:

> I had each shape name translated into the languages of the students that are in my classroom. Each shape was in English, Spanish, Khmer (Cambodian), Arabic and Albanian... When one of my students clicked a shape and heard the sound, he was excited and said, "It's my dad!" I could tell that they felt a genuine connection in the classroom. The ability to affirm these students' identities was so fulfilling... Having the students feel that their culture is important in the classroom was important to me. (Ella ePortfolio)

Ella was so passionate about integrating her students' languages into her teaching that she uploaded the completed computer game to her ePortfolio in spite of significant technical difficulties. Ella summed up her motivation and her success in a follow-up interview:

> After watching them interact with it, it was so much fun – it was really the drive for me... this was worth it to have kids see themselves in the classroom... like, "my language is important and it's not only important to me but it's important to my teachers.".... Bringing the parents into the classroom is huge. Like, to see these kids like, "That's my dad'! And like, 'that's me, that's my family."... At that point, I didn't even care about whether or not they were learning the shapes. It had nothing to do with the content at that point. It was the experience and it was a community of it. (Ella Interview)

Karla also centered her educational philosophy on connecting curriculum to students and their communities—"Much of student learning is based on their interest and involvement in the immediate community surrounding the school of my students" (Karla ePortfolio). Driven by this philosophy, Karla took her students to attend the nearest high school's homecoming parade. Karla reflected later:

> There were a variety of floats in the parade, including each club and team's float or performance. I was pleased to see the different clubs because many of them celebrated diversity of their races, cultures, genders, or ability levels. These floats showed my students the power

of pride and celebration of their differences. I learned this because when we reflected on the parade afterwards, the students talked about how surprised they were to see the many different clubs and that they didn't know so many groups existed. (Karla ePortfolio)

Cathy and Abby both conducted case studies of their students during their student teaching semester, each focusing on one student they would like to learn more about and support. Abby selected a girl who was "quiet, sweet, kind, and also happen[ed] to be an ELL student" for her case study (Abby, Video Reflection). In her reflection, Abby stated that this student's family came to the United States not long ago from Mexico and Abby was committed to "learning about her culture and her needs" and "providing all the support she needs." A few strategies Abby and her mentor teachers integrated into their teaching were pairing her with students who were both fluent in English and Spanish to help her navigate through the daily routines. She also provided "specific examples to guide her work and (offer) extra encouragement." At the same time, Abby expressed a deficit view of the student in a dehumanizing way, jumping to the conclusion that the student did not want to do her work, without exploring why she was hesitant to engage in hands-on activities:

One attribute of this student is that she is very cute so that she has charmed her friends to do a lot of her work for her. She doesn't enjoy cutting, pasting, drawing, or coloring. Some of her friends have chosen to pick up the slack for her. So one of the strategies I did is to provide very clear instructions so that I can clean up all the barriers to her understanding of the expectations… She plays coy when we encourage her to speak in front of her peers. She refuses to talk and she will do a deer and headlights act where she would have wide eyes and pretend and act like she had no idea what we were talking about. (Abby Video Reflection)

Helen and Craig were required to teach and record two lessons to demonstrate their ability to support all students, especially the ones from minoritized communities. In her educational philosophy statement, Helen pledged commitment to treating her students equally without further detail:

As a White woman, I do not feel a sense of being superior to anyone, especially my students. From day one, I feel as if I have done nothing but try and develop a connection with my students and treat them equally. If the student needs extra support in learning because of cultural differences, I will come up with as many strategies as I can to help them understand. (Helen Reflection)

It is important to note that Helen's statement also demonstrated a deficit view toward minoritized students, saying that students "need extra support in learning because of cultural differences," suggesting that some cultures do not value education in the same way that she did. In order to build the connection with her students, she designed a project for her students to complete a family tree activity with their family members. The students then presented their family tree in class. Through this activity, Helen learned that students in her class came from nine different countries and origins and spoke many different languages at home. She then posted the family trees on the wall in the classroom. Helen reflected that "this activity helped me learn more about the students, their backgrounds and heritages. I noticed that they were so proud to share their family origins!" (Helen Reflection).

These lessons and activities demonstrate that the participants tried to implement strategies in their actions such as inviting community members and parents from diverse communities to share their experiences and trying to get to know their students' cultural backgrounds. Nevertheless, taking a closer look at their teaching practices on a daily basis revealed gaps between their carefully prepared lessons and their interactions with minoritized students in unprepared circumstances. There was a particularly notable disconnect between how they carefully designed, prepared, and taught lessons as opposed to how they responded to unexpected situations arising in the classroom.

4.2 Backsliding Toward Dehumanizing and Criminalizing

In unscripted situations, all the White prospective teachers tended to backslide into systemic patterns of acting that reinforced dehumanizing and criminalizing of minoritized students through deficit labeling, interrogating/peer interrogating, policing/peer policing, body controlling, public shaming, zero tolerance, and segregating. They seldom used these

Table 4.1   Criminalizing and dehumanizing patterns of acting

Dehumanizing and criminalizing patterns of acting	Definition and examples
Deficit labeling	Referring to students in an essentialist way as violent, defiant, dangerous, disrespectful, difficult, bad, unable to learn, unwilling to learn, or low performing Example: "I know he can be defiant. I don't want him to hurt the two boys." "He is one year behind; he will always be."
Interrogating/ peer interrogating	Scolding, questioning, or reprimanding an individual or small group in an aggressive manner. These actions are similar to police interrogating suspects. This also happened when minoritized students were interrogated by their White peers. Example: "Why are you standing here? Why are you not doing anything?"
Policing/peer policing	Over-monitoring for negative behaviors such as socializing, standing up, not looking at the teacher/the board, or touching equipment without instructions. This also happened when minoritized students were policed by their White peers. Example: "What's your problem? Don't lie on the floor, especially with my computer. It's my computer. Do you have money to pay me if you break it?!"
Body controlling	Excessively demanding compliance with behavioral rules such as demanding silence, keeping eyes front, sitting perfectly facing front, and not moving from that position. Sometimes these rules were enforced by grabbing part of the students' body for control purposes. These hyper-controlling measures are similar to those employed in prison and other carceral institutions. Example: "Jamal, eyes on board. ... Jamal, keep your hands to yourself. ... Jamal, sit up still." The mentor teacher grabbed Jamal's arm and took him out of the classroom.
Disparate punishment	More frequently and/or severely punishing minoritized students compared with their White peers who committed the same infractions. Example: Juan was warned and punished but not his White tablemate even though the tablemate started the behavior first.
Public shaming	Belittling, criticizing, or shaming students in front of the whole class. Example: Telling the whole class about a student, "This is the second time you read the story. You should have known the story by heart. Shame. Sad."

(continued)

Table 4.1 (continued)

Dehumanizing and criminalizing patterns of acting	Definition and examples
Zero tolerance	Giving only one chance or no chance at all for students' minor infractions. Example: "So what we are doing is we give her one chance and then if she did it again, or didn't listen, or talk back, she was out."
Segregating	Separating students from the rest of class either socially or physically. This pattern of acting included both in-class segregation (taking learning opportunities away by positioning them away from the rest of the class, or denying them recess time or free choice time) and out-of-class segregation (from taking them momentarily into the hall to office referrals). These actions were often justified in terms of preserving the safety or learning opportunities of the other students. Example: Juan was taken away from his table and segregated from his peers. Jamal's teacher took him out of the classroom to prevent him from a "fight."

Adapted by the authors from Basile et al. (2019)

harsh actions toward White students in their classrooms, demonstrating a discipline disparity between minoritized students and their White peers. Most of these patterns of acting were congruent with those identified by Basile et al. (2019), who categorized five criminalizing practices toward boys of color: "hyper-policing and over-monitoring, controlling the body, interrogating, labeling, disparate punishment" (p. 15). Table 4.1 summarizes the eight patterns of acting we observed with examples from our observations; the definitions of the first five categories were adapted from Table 4.1 in Basile et al. (2019, p. 18) with examples from the cases reported in this book.

Our data triangulation demonstrates that these patterns of acting were driven by their habits of mind discussed in Chap. 3, forming a vicious and self-fulfilling cycle that perpetuated the historically established practices of dehumanizing and criminalizing minoritized students (Fig. 4.1).

In Chap. 3, we discussed the habits of mind that Abby and her mentor teacher had toward Jamal, the Black boy in their first-grade classroom. Earlier in this chapter, we also discussed how Abby described the girl who had recently moved to the United States from Mexico in a deficit and dehumanizing way. Intensive classroom observations further revealed that

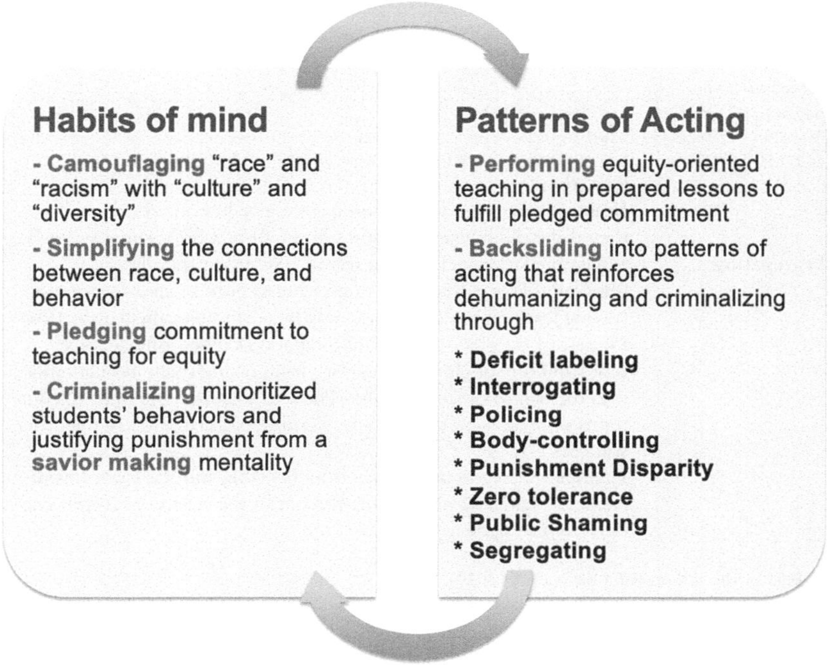

Habits of mind

- **Camouflaging** "race" and "racism" with "culture" and "diversity"

- **Simplifying** the connections between race, culture, and behavior

- **Pledging** commitment to teaching for equity

- **Criminalizing** minoritized students' behaviors and justifying punishment from a **savior making** mentality

Patterns of Acting

- **Performing** equity-oriented teaching in prepared lessons to fulfill pledged commitment

- **Backsliding** into patterns of acting that reinforces dehumanizing and criminalizing through

* **Deficit labeling**
* **Interrogating**
* **Policing**
* **Body-controlling**
* **Punishment Disparity**
* **Zero tolerance**
* **Public Shaming**
* **Segregating**

Fig. 4.1 The vicious cycle of habits of mind and patterns of acting

her habits of mind, primarily based on this deficit framework, directly impacted the actions she had in interacting with minoritized students. In one observation of Abby, the students were doing small group and independent work in various stations across the classroom. Jamal was in the group that was given the Nook Book to play math games, but he seemed to have trouble logging onto the Nook Book. Abby was walking around the classroom to check how students worked but she did not ask Jamal why he was not working on his Nook Book. Finally Jamal got the Nook Book working by himself. He sat down in the middle of a long bench in the classroom where two White boys were sitting at the two ends of the bench. As soon as Jamal sat down, the two White boys ran away, one of them yelling "Why are you sitting here? I don't want to sit with you." A couple of minutes later, it was time to transition to another station. Jamal did not spend much time on his Nook Book to play the math game he wanted to. Interestingly, when a new group of kids started to work on the

Nook Books, a White girl seemed to struggle with the Nook Book too. Abby knelt down one knee next to the girl and helped her get the Nook Book to work—something she had not done with Jamal.

In another observation, Abby was teaching a math lesson. One activity was reading the time on a clock. Jamal was the first to read and he did it correctly. After he was done, he walked to the middle of the classroom to wait for the other students to finish. A minute later, the mentor teacher walked to Jamal and asked: "Jamal, why are you standing here? You should line up to read the time." Jamal answered quietly, "I'm done." The mentor teacher walked away. Jamal started to line up to go to music. Since he was the first to complete the clock-reading task, he stood close to the door. Two White boys finished their clock-reading task and started lining up as well. Seeing that Jamal was in the front close to the door, the two boys interrogated him using a tone similar to the one the mentor teacher had used earlier, demanding: "Why are you here? You aren't doing anything!" Jamal did not respond, but the mentor teacher came over and said, "Jamal, you should line up to read the clock." Jamal looked confused but he did not protest. He lined up and did the clock reading task again and he read it correctly; Abby did not tell him that he did the task already. Jamal walked quickly back, trying to get to where he had been standing in line to go to music. The two boys who interrogated him earlier pushed him and yelled, "You're not supposed to be here!" Abby came over, holding one of Jamal's arms and said, "Jamal, you don't want to fight." At this point, the mentor teacher came over and took Jamal over from Abby. She grabbed Jamal by his right arm and took him out to the hallway.

After each observation, Katrina interviewed Abby and the mentor teacher, asking them their thoughts about Jamal and the interactions between him and the other children in the classroom. When asked about the behavior of the two boys running away from Jamal when Jamal sat down between them, their response was that Jamal was behind, would not work on his own, and the boys ran away from him in order to protect their own time. They concluded that nothing could be done to help him catch up with his classmates:

Mentor Teacher: Oh, they ran away because they knew that Jamal did not want to work on his own.

Abby: Yes they were afraid that Jamal was going to ask them to play the Nook Book for him.

Mentor Teacher:	They were trying to protect their time. They were trying to make good use of their time to play their math game so that they can be prepared for the MAP test.
Researcher:	I noticed that Jamal struggled to get the Nook Book working. Is there anything that can be done to help?
Abby:	We have been working hard to support him. There's nothing that can be done because the Nook Book has no password.
Researcher:	After Jamal finally got into the math game, he did not complete many math problems. Fifteen minutes are so fast before they have to move to another activity.
Mentor Teacher:	Jamal has to work on his own. We cannot do anything for him....like we cannot lower the level of the game just for him.
Researcher:	What can be done to help him?
Mentor Teacher:	I am not sure what can be done. **He is one year behind and he will always be** (emphasis the authors')
Abby:	(Nodding) Definitely.

When asked why Jamal was sent out of the classroom during the line up, Abby and the mentor teacher responded in a way similar to their earlier assumptions about Jamal, which was that Jamal was defiant and dangerous.

Mentor Teacher:	Abby, I am glad you caught him right away before he launched a fight.
Abby:	I know he can be defiant. I don't want him to hurt the two boys.
Researcher:	It looked like the other two boys started to criticize and push Jamal.
Mentor Teacher:	Jamal tends to be the troublemaker. He likes to cut into lines and that's why they were telling him not to do that.

Apparently, what they said about "nothing can be done" to help Jamal on the Nook Book was not true for other students because Abby helped another (White) girl get working on the Nook Book. In the incident of lining up, Abby and her mentor teacher criminalized Jamal by policing his body even though he did not engage in a fight. As a matter of fact, the two White boys interrogated him and pushed him. Without asking both sides about what happened, they assumed Jamal was the one who needed to be policed. Both Abby and the mentor teacher punished Jamal because of their distorted assumptions about him being dangerous and defiant. They segregated Jamal from the class in order to prevent the two White boys from being "hurt." During this process, Abby and her mentor teacher's deficit and criminalizing habits of mind about Jamal and their patterns of acting that incorporated policing, interrogating, and segregating interacted with each other, contributing to a vicious cycle of distorted habits of mind leading to inequitable actions. It is important to point out here that by criminalizing and punishing Jamal's behaviors in front of the entire classroom, Abby and her mentor teacher also served as a model for their White students. In both incidents, the White students questioned, interrogated, and policed Jamal. As teachers in the classroom, they both defended the White students. These incidents provided examples of "intergenerational socialization and lineage" (Bryan, 2017, p. 345), the perpetuation of discrimination and criminalization of minoritized people and the concomitant training of a new generation of White people to police the boundaries of Whiteness.

Let's turn our lens to Cathy, who conducted her student teaching in the same school as Abby. Cathy was placed in a kindergarten classroom. There was a Latino boy, Juan, in the class and similar to Abby's treatment of Jamal, Cathy called out Juan constantly for discipline purposes. During one observation of a math lesson, Juan was sitting with a White boy at the same table. The table was set in such a way that the White boy was facing the front, and Juan was not directly facing the front. When Cathy explained the procedures for a geoboard activity in which students would use rubber bands to make shapes, she called Juan's name multiple times for his attention without thinking that Juan was not facing the front where she stood to teach. After giving the instructions, Cathy told the class that she needed somebody to deliver rubber bands to the tables. Juan raised his hand enthusiastically but he was not called on to help. After his table got rubber bands, the White boy started to pull a rubber band and aimed at Juan and then let it go. The rubber band landed on Juan's shoulder and he started to giggle. The White boy did it again. Juan giggled again. Cathy heard it and warned Juan to be quiet. The White boy made a face and shot the rubber band at Juan again. This time, Juan picked up the rubber band and shot it back at the White boy. Cathy happened to see what Juan did, came over to him, and said: "Juan, you have been disruptive." Cathy then asked Juan to walk over to the front and sit next to the teacher's table. The White boy made a face again. Throughout the activity, Juan was segregated from the rest of his class, sitting there by himself, and lost the opportunity to participate in the classroom activities.

Now we turn to Craig's classroom. Craig was placed in a third-grade classroom for his field experience. As mentioned in Chap. 3, Craig described an African American boy, Malik, as "aggressive and defiant." In one class, Malik was talking to his tablemates. Craig gave him a verbal warning by calling his name. When he talked again, Craig took away his recess time. When a similar situation happened with a White student who was talking, Craig first gave him a verbal warning as well, but when the boy talked again, Craig walked up to him, patted his back gently, and quietly said "get back to your work." When Malik talked the third time, Craig's mentor teacher grabbed his arm and asked him to go to the back of the classroom. Malik waved his arm and protested, "I'm not going to go," and started to cry. The mentor teacher said, "No, Malik, you're angry" and took him out of the classroom to "calm down." The discipline logic of Craig and his mentor was directly linked to their assumptions about Malik being aggressive and defiant so that he needed to be punished, either through segregating him from the class or taking his recess time away.

After this field experience semester, while taking the rest of courses to fulfill the licensure requirements, Craig was hired by the school district as a third grade teacher in a school with 95% of students from the local Hispanic community. In an interview, Craig expressed that the students in the school needed "strict discipline" because they came from a community where parents had limited education and worked in low income jobs. He believed that students from these communities had no books to read and no parents to cook for them. He therefore believed that they were "not independent" and their behavior was "wild" and "out of control." During classroom observations, it quickly became clear that Craig's habits of mind guided his actions, with his teaching focusing on technical efficiency and him constantly yelling at the students harsh phrases such as "Go, go, go! Do not waste my time!" Craig constantly disciplined his students through name calling, labeling, public shaming, and threatening. During one observation, Craig introduced three students to Katrina, saying "I have these students who are the low students. I will work with them at the table to do reading intervention." A moment later, Craig was talking to the three students: "What are you guys doing? Why are you so slow? Why did it take you more than five minutes to find your reading package?"

In another lesson observation, Craig asked the students to find a partner and share the story they just read. He walked around the room and found a pair of students not sharing much. He asked the whole class to stop and publicly shamed the student:

Craig: You were not sharing anything.

Student: Yes I did.

Craig: For whatever reason, I didn't hear you share the story. I heard only three words. It's impossible to share the story in only three words. This is the second time you read the story. You should have known the story by heart. Shame. Sad. Now, go find another partner, and share your story.

At the end of the school day, the students were lining up to return their laptops to the stand in the classroom. One student was lying down on the floor with the laptop next to him on the floor. Craig immediately interrogated the student, saying: "What's your problem? Don't lie on the floor, especially with my computer. It's my computer. Do you have money to pay me if you break it?" After the class, Craig responded to Katrina's question about his overall experience in the school, demonstrating the deficit-based and savior-making habits of mind we discussed in Chap. 3:

I love them. They are from the neighborhood around here so their levels are low and they are less independent readers. They need structures and rules. The whole school is very well structured. I'm not the only teacher who implements strict structures. You've seen it–that student was lying on the floor with the computer. If I don't implement the structures, they will jump on the desks and do all sorts of things. That's why you see I'm very structured and I don't waste time. I don't let them waste time so they can achieve. They are much better behaved now. (Craig, Interview)

Now let us revisit Judy's classroom. As part of her equity unit on celebrations of light during her student teaching semester, Judy invited Katrina to give a guest lesson on the celebration of light based on her cultural background. This lesson followed previous lessons on Kwanzaa and Hanukkah. When Katrina arrived, Judy and her mentor teacher pulled her to the corner and said, "We have to warn you that we have a difficult child in the classroom. If you feel there is any problem, please let us know and we'll take her out." The "difficult" child was Olivia, mentioned earlier as the only African American student in the class. Judy and her mentor teacher knew that Olivia had no prior schooling experience and little understanding of classroom routines and behavioral expectations when she joined the class in the middle of the semester. During Katrina's presentation, Olivia showed no signs of problematic behavior. She was engaged in the activities and encouraged more hesitant students to participate.

At the end of the day, students were given free choice time before going home. Each student was allowed to choose from activities such as painting, playing puzzles, drawing, and decorating lampshades. Olivia selected painting. Students were supposed to put on the "artist" t-shirt before painting to protect themselves. Olivia did not do this. She was very excited about painting, creating an image of the mentor teacher. Then she painted an image of a cat and proudly asked several other students to look at her work. However, the mentor teacher considered this behavior disruptive and took her out of the classroom. Olivia ended the day—just as Judy and the mentor teacher predicted earlier—segregated from the class as a "difficult child." A few days later, in a conversation with Judy, Katrina asked what she thought of Olivia. Judy again labeled Olivia as "defiant." When asked about the strategies she used in teach Olivia, Judy's response invoked zero tolerance:

> So what we are doing is we give her one chance and then if she did it again, or didn't listen, or talk back, she was out. But I think she needed the consequence; otherwise she would walk over you. (Judy, Interview)

Rather than helping Olivia learn the routines, Judy and her mentor teacher implemented zero tolerance—"we give her one chance"—segregating her from the rest of the class when she erred. As mentioned in the findings on habits of mind, Judy discussed Olivia at some length in her interviews, demonstrating fair knowledge of the student's personal circumstances. At the same time, she justified the punitive, exclusionary behavior management applied to Olivia by presenting her behavior as deliberate, anti-authoritarian, and "cultural." This attitude demonstrates that her articulated commitment on social justice and equity did not translate to an awareness of educational inequity built around punishment and segregation in the classroom, nor did it transform inequitable actions toward minoritized students such as Olivia.

We mentioned earlier that Ella demonstrated much dedication to integrating the funds of knowledge from her students' families into her third-semester math shape unit. In the fourth semester, Ella was placed in a first-grade classroom. Ella and another prospective teacher placed in the fifth-grade classroom of the same school decided to address inter-age-group bullying by having students in both classes collaborate on skits about bullying. During one observation, Ella's first graders and her peer's fifth graders worked together to perform different bullying scenarios. The performance lasted about 35 minutes and was followed by a post-teaching conference with the university supervisor. During the debriefing, Ella and her partner explained to their supervisor why they designed this performance; and the supervisor praised them on their classroom management and the transitions between activities. He further praised them for their students' engagement. Ella's peer expressed agreement by saying "even the ones who could have been very inappropriate and could have crossed the line participated well." The supervisor then asked Ella if the lesson fit into her goal of building a classroom community to support all the students. Ella's response was "Oh, absolutely!"

> We think it went really well! All the students participated in the performance and they were all active. We're surprised that even Johnny, *who should not be included,* worked well! He could have messed things up! (Ella Post-Teaching Debrief, emphasis the authors')

Johnny was an African American fifth grader who apparently did well in this lesson. However, his good performance was considered "abnormal," and accidental, because his previous behaviors were considered unacceptable and therefore he was usually not included in class activities. Ella and her peer made the comments in such a natural way that they didn't even realize they were admitting to a systematic practice of excluding and segregating Johnny from the classroom, and thus limiting his opportunities to learn.

Finally, let us visit Karla's class. During one of the observations, we noticed an African American boy sitting alone far away from the rest of the class, and two other African American girls sitting together at a table. Karla did not call on any of these three students to answer questions nor did she interact with them when she walked around the classroom. During the post-teaching conference, Karla's supervisor asked why the African American boy was sitting by himself. Karla answered, "I don't know. He doesn't have behavioral problems. He might like sitting alone." When the supervisor commented that he always had his students have a special day such as a birthday to decide where to sit, and prompted Karla to find out if it was just a special day for the boy. Karla responded that "it's funny because he's been…. This has been at least two weeks." Karla then continued to defend her neglecting the student by saying "he also participates too …. He definitely …. So it's not that he's forgotten at the back." During this conversation, it was obvious that although Karla noticed that the student had been sitting alone away from the other students for at least two weeks, she either did not see it as a problem or she chose not to find out the reasons behind the segregation. The supervisor then shifted the conversation to the two African American girls:

Supervisor: The African American girls didn't often read along, but the white kids did. I don't know if this is just a random thing that happened today, or…. Like when you discussed, the two African American girls were left behind. Like in a push–pull sheet [a classroom assignment], they were just doing their own thing. This could just be a random thing, but if it's not, what does that say? Because I drew a picture kind of like the four White kids sitting together and the two African American girls were just kind of playing in the corner. What were your thoughts about that?

Karla: Well, actually, the thing is…. Okay, one of them is…. She came in last week, on
Monday, and she is kind of a bad influence on the other girls. The bigger one is new, and the smaller one, like, is the top reader in the class, top student, like I mean really.

Supervisor: Why don't you sit down with her? If you noticed that this new girl is bringing
the girl down, have a talk with the girl, the sooner
the better.

Karla: [My mentor teacher] mentioned that too…. She's not a bad girl. She's just way more social, she is a first grader [in terms of her education level, not in terms of her age], so she's…[trails off], but she's definitely bringing the other girls to the misbehavior level that they haven't been before.

In this conversation, the supervisor tried to prompt Karla to reflect on why the two African American girls were not participating in the class. Instead of reflecting on how her teaching might have some impact on their disengagement, Karla blamed the new student as a bad influence on the other girl and therefore making the two African American girls, especially the new one, responsible for the situation. Karla's habits of mind about the new African American student fit with long-standing socially distorted assumptions about African American students (Delpit, 2012; Howard, 2010; Irvine, 1990; Milner IV et al., 2018), leading her to segregate them within the classroom by simply ignoring them, and thus denying them the opportunity to learn.

4.3 Problematizing the Patterns of Acting

The patterns of acting of prospective teachers revealed through the analysis above indicate that our participants made performative efforts in their required assignments to prove that they were able to support all students in their classrooms with cultural awareness. For example, one goal of Ella's computer shape game was to break the barrier between formal schooling and home life, embracing students' identities and valuing her students' feelings about schooling. Similarly, Judy implemented the unit on equity by introducing different celebrations her students' families practiced because she wanted to include "the students' lives and also give them an opportunity to learn about lesser known celebrations" (Judy ePortfolio). Helen also made an effort to learn about her students' cultures and heritages through a family tree project.

However, our observations and interviews show limited evidence that the participants actually transformed their fundamentally deficit-oriented assumptions about minoritized students even though they conducted those performances of equity. Most concerning is the backsliding in which, in unscripted situations, the participants simply followed the lead of their cooperating teachers and placement schools. For example, Abby's patterns of acting through policing, segregating, and punishing Jamal showed us that her reflections on valuing cultural diversity, pledging commitment to social justice and equity failed to trigger transformation in either her understanding of racism or her actions of racial discrimination. In a real classroom situation, she was unable to reflect critically on her habits of mind about Jamal as a "dangerous and defiant" student and she defended and justified her inequitable practices toward Jamal based on her distorted assumptions. Judy's story also demonstrated the complications of racism that can occur in field placement. Although Judy's ePortfolio reflections indicated significant awareness of Olivia's home circumstances and her unfamiliarity with school routines, she showed no effort to challenge the problematic zero tolerance practices in punishing Olivia, nor did she link this practice to the historic over-disciplining of minoritized students. Karla failed to question her assumptions about diversity, segregating students of color within her classroom by ignoring their existence and denying them educational opportunities even though they were "included" in the classroom. This significant finding of disparities between prospective teachers' self-claimed commitment to equity pledged in their written reflection and the backsliding actions of dehumanizing and criminalizing minoritized students points to the importance for teacher educators to pay special attention to prospective teachers' classroom practice. As previous research (Cochran-Smith et al., 2015; Liu, 2020) demonstrated, teacher educators need to go beyond using prospective teachers' reflection and self-selective examples as evidence to understand prospective teachers' practice. Longitudinal observations such as those shown in this book, though time consuming, provide invaluable opportunities for teacher educators to learn about prospective teachers' learning process and transformation (or not) and, equally importantly, opportunities to critically reflect on the efficacy of teacher educators' own practices and make transformative changes at both individual and program levels.

The backsliding patterns of acting discussed in this chapter demonstrate the processes of labeling, interrogating, threatening, policing, and body controlling in criminalizing and dehumanizing minoritized students. These patterns reinforce what Basile et al. (2019) found in their study of dehumanizing and criminalizing students of color. Notably, our triangulated data analysis demonstrated that the White prospective teachers' patterns of acting were closely linked to deficit-based habits of mind regarding their minoritized students. These deficit habits of mind, especially the criminalizing and savior-making ones, served as rationale to justify their racist patterns of acting such as segregating, policing, and body controlling because the White prospective teachers believed that these actions were "good" for them and enhanced the "safety" of the White students. This vicious self-fulfilling cycle of habits of mind and patterns of acting needs to be recognized and addressed by teacher educators.

In addition to criminalizing students of color, our research revealed a sharp disparity between prospective teachers' patterns of acting toward minoritized students and White students. This finding aligns with other studies on racial disparities in classroom discipline (Annamma et al., 2019; Basile et al., 2019; Bryan, 2017; Milner IV et al., 2018). As CRT scholars have noted repeatedly, African American students are disproportionately pushed out from class and school for minor infractions (Skiba et al., 2011). It is clear in our findings that prospective teachers and their mentor teachers punished minoritized students harsher and more frequently than their White peers even though their behaviors were similar. These patterns of acting showed up again and again in the classrooms of Abby, Craig, and Cathy. Students such as Jamal, Juan, and Olivia were treated with zero tolerance (Skiba & Petterson, 1999; Solari & Balshaw, 2007) and punished through exclusionary practices such as loss of recess time, sitting away from the rest of the class, and being taken out to the hallway while their White peers were given less severe discipline such as verbal warnings and gentle redirection. Their experiences speak to the daily reality of minoritized students' lives, and echo disparities reported by Williford et al. (2021).

Our results also demonstrate that White peers policed and interrogated minoritized students; these problematic behaviors were justified and endorsed by the White prospective teachers and their mentor teachers. This was especially visible in the case of Jamal, who was repeatedly interrogated and punished by his White peers. This finding confirms Bryan's (2017) observation that White students learn to criminalize their peers of color by observing their teachers—"particularly as they observe how their White teachers disproportionately target them for minor and subjective school disciplinary infractions" (p. 326).

We would like to point out that in all the incidents we observed, the White prospective teachers' mentor teachers played an important role in building a toxic classroom culture by either taking the lead or assisting in the actions of dehumanizing and criminalizing. We do want to acknowledge the power hierarchy between mentor teachers and prospective teachers during field placement (Anderson, 2007; Gao et al., 2019; Liu, 2020) that could potentially motivate the prospective teachers to simply follow their mentor teachers' patterns of acting. For example, Gao et al. (2019) revealed that prospective teachers followed the deficit tone of their mentor teachers in describing minoritized students. This is certainly true in the incidents such as Abby and her mentor teacher and Craig and his mentor teacher in describing Jamal and Malik and their cooperative actions in segregating and policing them. Based on these findings, we strongly argue that teacher education programs need to take deliberate and transformative actions to find classroom mentor teachers who are able to model equity-oriented and anti-racist teaching in order to dismantle the multi-generational legacy of violence against minoritized students. This is a long-term human project, as Toni Morrison (2017) called it, "to remain human and to block the dehumanization and estrangement of others" (p. 37). Otherwise, White prospective teachers will learn to "teach in the shadow" (Hollins, 2019, p. 15) of White supremacy, perpetuating the intergenerational criminalizing and dehumanizing of these students.

Finally, it is worth noting that the participants in this study were almost all White women, reflecting the national demographics of the elementary teacher corps as a whole. Multiple researchers have noted the linkage between "White hegemonic femininity" (Bryan, 2020) and White fragility (DiAngelo, 2018) and the criminalizing of minoritized students (Bryan, 2021; Deliovsky, 2010; Leonardo & Boas, 2013; Tyson, 2017). Framing minoritized students—male and female—as a particular threat to White women thus links school discipline with a long and bloody history in the United States of lynching, colonialism, and mass incarceration (Irvine-Baker et al., 2022). We find, in short, that although prospective teachers were able to perform in required assignments and activities with elements from culturally relevant and sustaining teaching, their planned actions, albeit well-intentioned, did not lead to transformative learning in their future teaching, especially when the response to unexpected events backslid on unexamined assumptions. Exposure to the concepts of diversity, multicultural education, and even CRT in short-term coursework alone did not fundamentally transform prospective teachers' assumptions about race and racism. As a result, their actions in the classroom tended to repeat or reinforce long standing racist and oppressive patterns.

4.4   CONCLUSION

Without a doubt, the creation of new knowledge is critically important. However, in addition to the creation of new knowledge, we must remember that the conduct of research, though necessary, is not sufficient to address social problems, mitigate inequalities, or advance innovative methods of instruction …. We know that we must do more than "know" in order to remain relevant and responsive to the challenges facing education in the 21st century. (Ball, 2012, p. 284)

Our findings based on the longitudinal study of White prospective teachers helped reveal problematic habits of mind and patterns of acting regarding race and racism, and crucially pointed to many of them knowing how they should think and act, but not being able to take the next step and change their worldviews and behaviors. However, prospective teachers are hardly alone in this predicament: We teacher educators also have a history of researching problems, proposing solutions, then returning to our research and leaving the heavy work of making real change to someone else. This needs to stop; we have the knowledge, now we need to act. Here we draw on Arnetha Ball's (2012) call for action during her AERA presidential talk in 2012, in which she asserted that gaining knowledge about what is not working is not enough: Taking action to transform what does not work is imperative. We argue that in addition to discovering failures, teacher educators must take emancipatory action, stimulating transformative and generative change in teacher education for educational equity for minoritized students (Liu & Ball, 2019). With this understanding, teacher educators need to help prospective teachers develop awareness of how their habits of mind are developed and shaped by a White supremacist system and how their patterns of acting, driven by these habits of mind, reinscribe the social, political, and emotional violence that produces school-based trauma (Duane, 2023). Prospective teachers need to be further supported in searching for alternative and generative solutions to transform their practices and therefore the oppressed and criminalized experiences of minoritized students. We echo the call from other researchers that teacher preparation must include coursework on (a) understanding White privilege and discipline disparity, and (b) transformative pedagogy to support generative actions to disrupt the dehumanizing and criminalization of non-White students (Basile et al., 2019; Fenning & Rose, 2007). In the next chapter, we step back from the details of prospective teachers' habits of mind and patterns of acting to consider the issues involved in transforming both individuals and institutions, and the requirements we have identified for successful transformation toward anti-racist education.

REFERENCES

Anderson, D. (2007). The role of cooperating teachers' power in student teaching. *Education, 128*(3), 307–323.

Annamma, S. A., Anyon, Y., Joseph, N., Farrar, J., Greer, E., Downing, B., & Simmons, J. (2019). Black girls and school discipline: The complexities of being overrepresented and understudied. *Urban Education, 54*(2), 211–242.

Ball, A. F. (2012). Presidential address: To know is not enough: Knowledge, power, and the zone of generativity. *Educational Researcher Journal, 41*(8), 283–293.

Basile, V., York, A., & Black, R. (2019). Who's the one being disrespectful? Understanding and deconstructing the criminalization of elementary school boys of color. *Urban Education, 57*(9), 1592–1620.

Bryan, N. (2017). White teachers' role in sustaining the school-to-prison pipeline: Recommendations for teacher education. *Urban Review, 49*(2), 326–345.

Bryan, N. (2020). Shaking the bad boys: Troubling the criminalization of black boys' childhood play, hegemonic white masculinity and femininity, and the school playground-to-prison pipeline. *Race Ethnicity and Education, 23*(5), 673–692.

Bryan, N. (2021). *Toward a BlackBoyCrit pedagogy: Black boys, male teachers, and early childhood classroom practices*. Routledge.

Cochran-Smith, M., Villegas, A. M., Abrams, L., Chavez-Moreno, L., Mills, T., & Stern, R. (2015). Critiquing teacher preparation research: An overview of the field II. *Journal of Teacher Education, 56*(2), 109–121.

Deliovsky, K. (2010). *White femininity: Race, gender, and power*. Fernwood Publishing.

Delpit, L. (2012). *Multiplication is for white people: Raising expectations for other people's children*. New Press.

DiAngelo, R. (2018). *White fragility: Why it's so hard to talk to white people about racism*. Beacon Press.

Duane, A. (2023). School-based trauma: A scoping review. *The Journal of Trauma Studies in Education, 2*(2), 102–124.

Fenning, P., & Rose, J. (2007). Overrepresentation of African American students in exclusionary discipline: The role of school policy. *Urban Education, 42*(6), 536–559.

Gao, S., Liu, K., & McKinney, M. (2019). Learning formative assessment in the field: Analysis of reflective conversations between preservice teachers and their classroom mentors. *International Journal of Mentoring and Coaching in Education, 8*(3), 197–216.

Hollins, E. R. (2019). *Teaching to transform urban schools and communities: Powerful pedagogy in practice*. Routledge.

Howard, T. C. (2010). *Why race and culture matter in schools: Closing the achievement gap in America's classrooms*. Teachers College Press.

Irvine, J. J. (1990). *Black students and school failure: Policies, practices and prescriptions.* Greenwood Press.

Irvine-Baker, A., Canfield, A., & Reyes, C. (2022). Liberating Black youth across the gender spectrum through the deconstruction of the White femininity / Black masculinity duality. In C. L. Bust & L. K. Semprevivo (Eds.), *Queering criminology in theory and praxis: Reimagining justice in the criminal legal system and beyond* (pp. 159–174). Bristol University Press.

Leonardo, Z., & Boas, E. (2013). Other kid's teachers: What Children of Color learn from White women and what this says about race, whiteness, and gender. In M. Lynn & A. Dixson (Eds.), *Handbook of Critical Race Theory in education.* Routledge Press.

Liu, K. (2020). *Critical reflection for transformative learning.* Springer.

Liu, K., & Ball, A. F. (2019). Critical reflection and generativity: Toward a framework of transformative teacher education for diverse learners. *Review of Research in Education, 43*(1), 68–105.

Mezirow, J. (Ed.). (1990). *Fostering critical reflection in adulthood: A guide to transformative and emancipatory learning.* Jossey-Bass.

Milner, H. R., Cunningham, H. B., Delale-O'Connor, L., & Kestenberg, E. G. (2018). *"These kids are out of control:" Why we must reimagine "classroom management" for equity.* Corwin.

Morrison, T. (2017). *Being or becoming the stranger: The origin of others.* Harvard University Press.

Skiba, R. J., Horner, R. H., Chung, C., Rausch, M. K., May, S., & Tobin, T. (2011). Race is not neutral: A national investigation of African American and Latino disproportionality in school discipline. *School Psychology Review, 40*, 85–107.

Skiba, R. J., & Petterson, R. (1999). The dark side of zero tolerance: Can punishment lead to safe schools? *Phi Delta Kappan, 80*(5), 372–382.

Solari, F. P., & Balshaw, J. E. M. (2007). Outlawed and exiled: Zero tolerance and second-generation race discrimination in public schools. *North Carolina Central Law Journal, 29*, 147–191.

Tyson, T. (2017). *The blood of Emmett Till.* Simon and Schuster.

Williford, A., Alamos, P., Whittaker, J., & Accavitti, M. (2021). *Who's left out of learning? Racial disparities in teachers' reports of exclusionary discipline strategies beyond suspensions and expulsions.* (EdWorkingPaper: 21-472). Annenberg Institute at Brown University: https://doi.org/10.26300/pep2-w676

CHAPTER 5

Toward Anti-Racist Teacher Education

Time has played an invaluable role in our own journey as researchers and teacher educators; the very length of our engagement with teacher education, and the way research and teaching have worked together to bring us to the insights offered in this book provides a guide for teachers as well. In this chapter we briefly walk through the path the three of us have taken to develop as teacher educators. We then use that path as an example of longitudinal praxis in teacher education, drawing lessons from the ways in which our goals as teacher educators transformed over time to suggest similar directions for prospective teachers preparing to educate students from minoritized communities. The outlines of a transformed teacher education program are fleshed out in Chap. 6 using our own programmatic innovations as examples.

5.1   GROWING TOWARD ANTI-RACIST TEACHER EDUCATION

In Chap. 2 we introduced the idea of developing anti-racist education as the goal of transformative teacher education. The resulting teacher education programs themselves must be anti-racist with courses, field experiences, and professional development opportunities designed intentionally and systematically to prepare educators to recognize how racism operates

K. Liu et al., *Preparing White Teachers for Anti-Racist Education*, https://doi.org/10.1007/978-3-031-73534-9_5

in educational settings, and then to actively address racism and systemic inequities in their teaching practice, curriculum, and school communities (Lipsitz. 1995; Shim, 2018). Anti-racist teacher education also requires teacher educators to implement and model practices that create equitable learning opportunities to acknowledge, embrace, and sustain the literacies, practices, and languages of students from non-dominant communities (Ladson-Billings, 1995; Milner, 2010, 2023; Paris, 2012). This thorough-going consistency and coherence at all levels of a teacher education program is vital to prepare anti-racist teachers (Joyner, 2024). The first steps of anti-racist teacher education must therefore concentrate on the critical examination of racism in the context of schools, teachers, and teaching and related systems and structures (McKamey, 2020), promoting critical reflection on and analysis of racism, privilege, and power dynamics within education and society (Gadd, 2023; Muhammad, 2023). From there, anti-racist teacher education must pivot toward action, prospective teachers, mentor teachers, and teacher educators collaborating on ways in which to transform practices in light of the insights from critical reflection and analysis. Finally, educators must learn to integrate perspectives, voices, and materials from minoritized communities into their curriculum, instructional strategies, and the design of instructional materials. As Django Paris (2012) argued, this culturally relevant and sustaining approach has the potential to "perpetuate and foster—to sustain—linguistic, literate, and cultural pluralism as part of the democratic project of schooling" (p. 94). Therefore, teacher educators must work from the standpoint of culturally relevant and culturally sustaining pedagogies, providing robust learning and identity resources to support prospective teachers' development as anti-racist educators (Oamek, 2024).

At the same time, teacher educators must recognize and plan to circumvent the barriers to developing and implementing anti-racist teaching and teacher education (Aronson & Meyers, 2020). These barriers are a combination of the personal and the institutional, so prospective teachers and teacher educators must work together at both levels. Teacher educators have long noted the individual and collective resistance of many prospective teachers to the basic insights of CRT (Evans-Winters & Twyman Hoff, 2011; Matias et al., 2016), multicultural education (Estrada & Matthews, 2016; Greenman & Kimmel, 1995; LaDuke, 2009; Mildred & Zuñiga, 2004), culturally responsive and sustaining education (Chen et al., 2021), and anti-racist education (Matias & Mackey, 2016; Shim, 2018; St. Denis and Schick, 2003). Much of this resistance, as we discussed in Chap. 3, can be summarized as the denial of racism and privilege on the part of prospective teachers, often supported in these habits of mind by teacher educators, mentor teachers, and peers. There are also institutional barriers to developing and implementing anti-racist teacher education, including race-evasive curriculum, pedagogy, and research, as well as more subtle barriers described by Martell et al. (2024), such as state teaching and learning standards that enforce "silent" covenants protecting the privileges and sensibilities of White teachers, students, families, and political stakeholders in public education. Addressing these institutional barriers of course requires teachers educators challenge toxic habits of mind, but also dismanle racist patterns of acting, as we demonstrated in Chap. 4.

Clearly, teacher educators play a critical role in challenging and transforming systems of oppression and promoting social justice in education. By equipping teachers with the knowledge, skills, and dispositions to be anti-racist educators, these programs aim to create more equitable and inclusive learning environments where all students can thrive. Ladson-Billings (1995) states

> This work is important for its break with the cultural deficit or cultural disadvantage explanations which led to compensatory educational interventions. A next step for positing effective pedagogical practice is a theoretical model that not only addresses student achievement but also helps students to accept and affirm their cultural identity while developing critical perspectives that challenge inequities that schools (and other institutions) perpetuate. I term this pedagogy, culturally relevant pedagogy. (p. 469)

Elsewhere she explains

> Culturally relevant teaching views knowledge as something that is continuously re-created, recycled, and shared. (Ladson-Billings, 2009, p. 88)

Notions of anti-racism in education owe a great deal to the work of Sleeter (1995) who advanced multicultural education in teacher education, and anti-racist teaching has also been connected to the idea of abolitionist teaching (Love, 2019; Howard, 2010). Importantly, in many of his works, Milner (e.g., 2010, 2021, 2023) provided a thorough analysis of opportunity gaps that minoritized students of color encounter due to institutional structures, policies, and instructional practices through "color and race avoidance," "cultural conflicts," "the myth of meritocracy," "deficit thinking and low expectations," "context neutrality," and "structures and systems" (Milner, 2023, pp. 40–43). These opportunity gaps cause "academic, cognitive, social, affective, emotional, behavioral, and psychological challenges" for minoritized students of color (Milner, 2021, p. 10). Based on this critical analysis, Milner conceptualized frameworks of opportunity-centered teaching (2010, 2021) and opportunity-centered school leadership (2023), both of which provided us with theoretical and pedagogical guidance toward anti-racism, including

> cultivat[ing] relationships with young people, colleagues in schools, families, parents, community advocates, policymakers, and educational researchers… [using] community knowledge to inform practices…. advanc[ing] psychological and mental health among students, school personnel, families, and communities of the school…. converg[ing] the curriculum…. and push[ing] the curriculum to social action. (Milner 2023, pp. 51–54)

While anti-racist teaching, culturally relevant teaching, and culturally sustaining pedagogy share common goals of promoting equity and inclusion in education, they differ somewhat in their focus, strategies, and underlying principles. We have tried to honor these principles and traditions in our work and use what has been most helpful to us in our analysis.

The three authors of this book have worked together over several years while developing as anti-racist teacher educators across time and multiple spaces and places. Over the past dozen years, we have engaged in the process of identity construction, pedagogical development, and theoretical sophistication. When the study first started, and for two years, Katrina dedicated herself to intensive fieldwork with four prospective teacher participants, immersing herself in their teaching and learning environments through ongoing interviews and classroom observations. This immersive experience not only deepened her understanding of teacher education programs, courses, and field experiences in relation to preparing future teachers for equity and social justice, but more specifically, led her to deconstruct disparities between what prospective teachers articulated in their written reflection about their commitment to social justice and equity and what they actually did in their teaching to perpetuate the reality of racialized experiences of their students' of color (Tatum, 2017). An in-depth analysis of prospective teachers' written reflections while engaged in a teacher preparation program at a large Midwestern university revealed that the cultural factors that prospective teachers engaged while producing written reflections that would serve as evidence for the evaluation of their learning led the prospective teachers to *cherry pick* the positive aspects of their teaching and avoid talking about challenges or failures (Liu, 2011).

During this same period, Katrina and Michael started to collaborate at Midwestern University on a grounded theory study to explore the patterns of prospective teachers' written reflection. In this study we were able to notice habits of mind and patterns of acting among prospective and in-service teachers. This was revealed in a longitudinal study of prospective teachers' written reflections as well as their practices in classrooms. In this study, we used classic grounded theory (Glaser & Strauss, 1967; Glaser, 1978, 1998). The goal of a classic grounded theory study is to inductively construct a theory by discovering latent patterns in data; thus, when we conducted our initial study, we did not use an explicit theory or theoretical framework but sought instead to find patterns in the data and integrate them into a new theory. In this way, the theory is *grounded* in data.

This classic grounded theory analysis helped us see that prospective teachers tended to showcase or *sunshine* their teaching and learning experiences rather than reflect on them analytically and critically. In their reflections, prospective teachers sunshined their classroom activities by carelessly using academic buzzwords, whitewashing negative experiences by *downtoning* the importance of problems in their teaching, and *blameshifting* the responsibility for problems in their classrooms onto other actors (Thomas & Liu, 2012). In previous studies (Thomas & Liu, 2012; Liu, 2020), we found that some prospective teachers didn't want to portray themselves as incompetent or doing anything wrong because they needed to demonstrate that they met their program requirements and state standards for licensure purposes. In effect, they were not really able to be fully reflective. Instead, they reflected in positive ways on surface issues, bragging about their accomplishments. This performative "reflection" came about because they knew that they were being assessed, that there would be consequences for doing things "wrong." This knowledge of assessment created an evaluative and high-stakes environment in which few regrets would be expressed publicly, successes emphasized, and failures explained away or even ignored. In addition to revealing the general patterns of prospective teachers' reflection, we saw that the preservice teachers were talking about race in a race-evasive way and that was cause for concern.

Race Talk followed the sunshining pattern. In Race Talk reflection there is talk about diversity and race but never societal critique on issues related to these topics. Rather it is about how "I" the outsider teacher fit in and built trust among African Americans and immigrants. We suspect that it may be that mentioning African Americans involves some kind of sunshining. This is because it is a praiseworthy thing to do in the culture of teacher education and anthropology more generally since race is coupled with the notion of "at risk" and the promise of education to mitigate the problem of economic disadvantage. (Thomas & Liu, 2012, p. 318)

This finding prompted us to dig for the root causes of race-evasive talks and how to address them:

This kind of thinking allows the prospective teachers to bracket out experience in favor of imagination. It is good that they, at times, point out things that they feel they may have done wrong or could have done better. But there was almost never any discussion of socioeconomic conditions, historic realities, or larger issues at work. We may have inadvertently taught prospective teachers to focus on good intentions rather than on the problems that unfold in real life situations. (Thomas & Liu, 2012, p. 328)

In 2011, armed with the insights gained from this research, Katrina took on the role of a teacher educator in a rural, state university in the Midwest—Clear Lake University. Recognizing the need to address the performative and self-fulfilling nature of reflection coming from an evaluative culture using written reflection for assessment, she integrated strategies into her teaching such as dialogic learning and collaborative reflection (Liu, 2017) to support prospective teachers' engagement in meaningful conversations about race and racism in their habits of mind and patterns of acting. This non-evaluative and dialogic process helped White prospective teachers critically analyze their prior distorted assumptions about students from racially minoritized communities. Through collaborative reflection in a dialogic space, some White prospective teachers were able to implement some transformative solutions in their practice while avoiding the pitfalls of White fragility (DiAngelo, 2018). Nevertheless, as described in several cases in Chaps. 3 and 4, transformation was at best transitory, with prospective teachers backsliding toward deficit-models and the discriminatory practices that both stem from and support those models.

In 2015, a new chapter in Katrina's career unfolded when she transitioned to another teacher education program situated in a large urban-intensive (Milner, 2012) context in the Southwestern part of the United States, Desert View University. This move marked a significant shift in her focus toward preparing future teachers to teach for equity in urban contexts, drawing inspiration from literature on conceptualization of urban education (Hollins, 2019; Milner, 2010, 2012; Oakes et al., 2002), the school-to-prison pipeline (Annamma, 2017; Skiba et al., 2014), and the criminalization of students of color and institutional structures perpetuating inequity (Alexander, 2012; Basile et al., 2019; Bryan, 2017). Katrina reshaped her teaching philosophy, integrating critically reflective and generative practices that centered on culturally relevant and sustaining community-based teacher education (Alim & Paris, 2017). Recognizing the importance of dismantling systemic barriers, Katrina sought to support future educators with tools to challenge inequity and cultivate environments that fostered inclusivity and understanding. Michael, after moving to a different institution that is urban intensive (Milner, 2012), continued supervising and working with doctoral students to take deep analysis of cultural and policy factors that impact teacher education programs at the institutional levels that in turn impact teacher educators and prospective teachers' practices. As the standardized portfolio-based prospective teacher assessment program edTPA became an important nationwide approach, Michael chaired a doctoral student's dissertation that focused on how institutional cultures impacted the practices of edTPA implementation. Richard, also moved to an institute that is urban intensive, shifted his research more to music education and equity, using CRT as a theoretical lens to analyze inequity and White supremacy in music education and teacher education. He and Katrina, in collaboration with Arnetha Ball, integrated critical reflection and generative change into counter-narrative as a transformative methodology as well as a pedagogical tool in teacher education (e.g., Miller et al., 2020; Liu et al., 2023).

Since these early collaborations, the three of us have worked together as both researchers and teacher educators in multiple institutions but always with a focus on synergizing research and teaching. Our own journey of learning and becoming across time and space enabled our longitudinal research processes and results to inform our teaching, and our teaching to drive our research agenda. In this way, the results in this book represent how research informed our practices in teaching and supervising prospective teachers across time. At the same time, teaching serves as a venue for us to make efforts to advance teacher education research to inform teacher education programs. These experiences laid the foundation for principles that would guide our future endeavors as teacher educators. They also enabled us to see that our own experience growing as anti-racist researchers (e.g., Kendi, 2019) could facilitate the development of anti-racist approaches to teacher education using the insights we gain from critical self-reflection to help prospective teachers attain similar growth.

In the longitudinal study that forms the basis to this book, we turned away from grounded theory to analyze reflective artifacts, interviews, and observations and explicitly used existing theory as a lens for analysis, especially when examining the interactions between White prospective teachers and the minoritized students in their classrooms. A grounded theory may, in turn, offer a data-driven, concrete way to then engage in *grounded action* (Simmons, 2022; Simmons & Gregory, 2003). A theory provides a way to *background* some ideas and *foreground* others in data; we used the existing theoretical framework of CRT in a praxis emphasizing critical counter-narrative to foreground the presence of racism in our participants' experiences of school and schooling, and providing an entry point to conversations about Whiteness and White supremacy in teacher education in ways that go beyond more polarized discourses about race (Klein, 2020; Stovall, 2016). This theory-driven research generated the findings presented in Chaps. 3 and 4 which we then used to inform our practices to develop the outcomes we desired to see in preparing anti-racist teachers. Revising our pedagogy and curriculum to aim for those outcomes required us to create new tools to intervene in prospective teachers' learning so they would more consciously focus on issues of racism and White supremacy, and the results of these interventions then informed further research. In this way there has been a reciprocal relationship between (a) Theory and Research; (b) Intervention; and (c) Outcomes (Fig. 5.1).

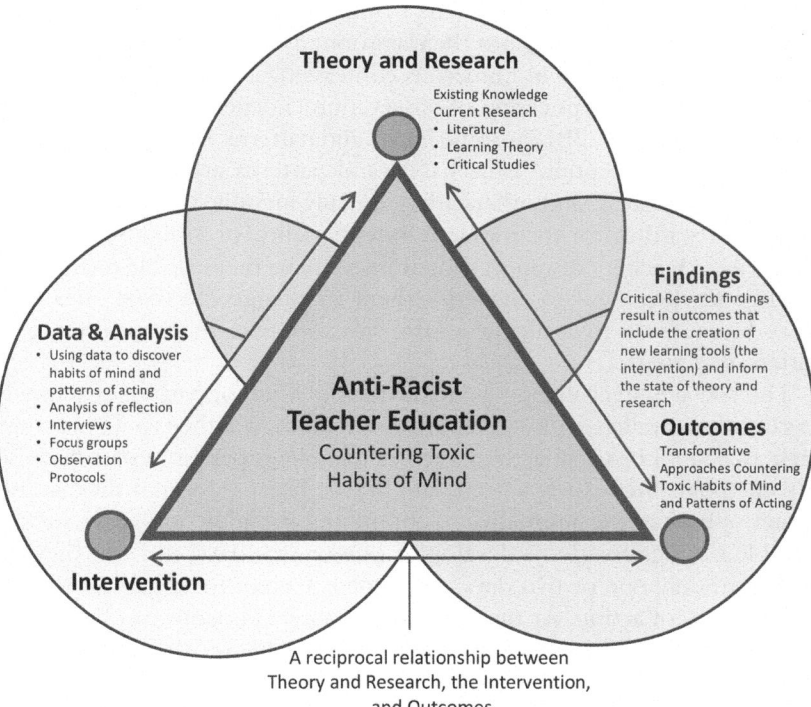

Fig. 5.1 Reciprocal relationships between theory and research, interventions, and outcomes

5.2 How Can We Challenge Toxic Habits of Mind and Patterns of Acting?

In the next chapter we discuss specific interventions we have developed in our own teacher education practice to leverage counter-narratives in the context of critical reflection for transformative learning. Here we address the intermediate level of the framework, addressing the issues that may arise in challenging prospective teachers' habits of mind and patterns of acting when attempting to develop and implement anti-racist teacher education.

Chapters 3 and 4 presented our analysis of White prospective teachers' habits of mind and patterns of acting with respect to race and racism. It is useful to remember that the habits of mind and patterns of acting that prospective teachers bring into the classroom do not come from nowhere but have been nurtured in numerous contexts by a combination of direct instruction, the apprenticeship of observation (Lortie, 1975), and teacher socialization (Bryan, 2017). Some habits and patterns are nurturing, some toxic, and some neutral; some habits and patterns are deliberately and consciously pursued, and others are essentially invisible to the prospective teacher. Regardless of their source, intentionality, or visibility, however, the goals of teacher education should be to make them visible to the prospective teachers, and to challenge them to change the toxic ones. But what does it mean to challenge a toxic habit of mind, to transform a toxic pattern of acting?

The first step in challenging a toxic habit of mind or pattern of acting is to consider parallels with addiction. Addictions, whether to a substance such as alcohol or to an activity such as gambling, persist in part because at some point they satisfy a need, and in part because, even if they are no longer satisfying, the alternative to continuing the addiction seems inconceivable. Addictions don't develop in one or two days, nor can they be broken in only one or two days; the same is true of toxic habits of mind and patterns of acting. At the same time, some addictions can be treated by replacing the once-satisfying activity with another activity that can once again satisfy the need originally addressed by the addiction—giving up smoking by switching to lollipops, for example. The same is true of toxic habits of mind and patterns of acting: When we understand why a toxic habit of mind or pattern of acting came about, we can often imagine an alternative that would address the underlying need without causing so much trauma to ourselves and those around us. For example, practices of punitive meritocracy in education, such as insisting that no one is perfect, and therefore refusing to give any student full marks, could reflect a need for control in the classroom that, in turn, stems from a fear of appearing to be an inexpert or ineffective teacher in a system that rewards neoliberal "efficiency" (Harvey, 2023). Recognizing the underlying fear and helping the teacher develop a greater sense of self-efficacy could allow them to relinquish the satisfaction they feel from denying students the grades they have earned.

A corollary to the connection with addiction is to be clear that maintaining toxic habits of mind or patterns of acting is not a sign of moral failing on the part of the prospective teacher. Toxic habits of mind and patterns of acting develop when there is an institutional environment that encourages and nurtures it, whether the assumptions underlying the habit of mind or patterns of acting originate in that institution or not. For example, the assumption of dangerousness that underlies the criminalization of Black schoolchildren does not originate in the schools themselves—it is a basic element in the stereotype of Blackness that permeates American society—but it certainly is encouraged and nurtured in schools. In fact, as Bryan (2017) observed, the toxic habits of mind and patterns of acting revolving around the danger of Blackness are not only passed from mentor teachers to prospective teachers but from both to the students in their classrooms. We saw in Chaps. 3 and 4 that Jamal and Olivia experienced interrogation and policing at the hands of their White classmates, who were essentially deputized by their teacher to enforce White supremacy in the classroom. This tutelage in racism depends upon the existence of anti-Blackness in American society, but then uses those existing habits of mind to make the patterns of acting seem normal, expected, and even rewardable.

5.3   The Importance of the Dialogic Space

With the awareness that toxic habits of mind and patterns of acting are not solely the fault of an individual but (like race itself) are socially and institutionally constructed and nurtured, it should be clear that challenging toxic habits of mind and patterns of acting must also happen on both the level of the individual and that of the institution. This means that counter-narrative, operating within the framework of critical reflection for transformative learning, has to happen in a *dialogic space* (Liu, 2017); it cannot be left for the individual prospective teacher to develop on their own in their placement, no matter how much their coursework has emphasized the importance of becoming an anti-racist educator. Developing counter-narrative within a dialogic space refers to understanding reflection as an act of intertextual analysis in which the preservice teacher's reflections are examined in relation to both other written texts and "social texts"—the authentic voices of students, family members, and colleagues (Liu, 2017, p. 3) with the goal of opening up narratives of learning beyond the narrow concerns of competence and control. When pursued in a dialogic space, critical reflection can more fully engage the complex work of teacher preparation, helping to identify (and ideally prevent) sunshining, blameshifting, and other performative actions that allow prospective teachers to avoid authentic reflection on issues of race and racism (Thomas & Liu, 2012).

The key element to critical reflection within a dialogic space, providing insight into toxic habits of mind and patterns of acting, is the use of counter-narratives, stories that run contrary to the established perspective, embodying the real-life experiences and voices of marginalized communities within schools and schooling. Elsewhere (Miller et al., 2020) we proposed the use of critical counter-narrative within a praxis of educational equity, stating

> Critical counter-narrative is a methodology for critically analyzing the racialized social reality in the education system and society by narrating the authentic lived experiences of people of color, searching for and acting upon emancipatory solutions, and transforming the educational system in order to provide equitable education for people of color. (p. 275)

Critical counter-narrative, used in a praxis for educational equity, is a potent pedagogical tool to help White preservice teachers recognize toxic habits of thought and patterns of acting with respect to racism and White supremacy (Miller et al., 2020). It may be used to first nurture a safe space for the transformation to occur for prospective teachers of color to share their experiences of society, schools, and schooling. These experiences can help White prospective teachers to link what they read (at a distance, distancing themselves as White people from racism) with what occurs in the real world among people of color. In a field placement setting, an important strategy to help White prospective teachers break away from toxic habits of mind and patterns of acting when working with minoritized students is learning directly from community members (Liu & Ball, 2019). As Zeichner and Payne (2013) observed, "while the role of school-based expertise is essential in teacher preparation, the role of expertise based in local communities is also important" (p. 11). Teachers may imagine that they understand their students because they see them daily in school, but this is unlikely absent serious engagement with the students' communities, as concrete knowledge of minoritized communities cannot come from traditional, university-based teacher education programs (Yuan, 2018, p. 13). There is a rising amount of research on preparing prospective teachers to work within communities in this way (Cochran-Smith & Villegas, 2015; Graue, 2005; Yuan, 2018; Zeichner et al., 2016). Murrell (2000) referred to the notion of the "community teacher" who develops the contextualized knowledge of culture, community, and identity of children and their families as the core of their teaching practice. Community teachers possess the "multicultural competence" they need for accomplished practice in the communities they teach. Community teachers are individuals who typically live and work in the same under-resourced urban neighborhoods and communities where students from diverse backgrounds live and go to school. (p. 340)

Zeichner et al. (2016) offered a three-part typology of teacher-family-community relations in teacher education to distinguish the epistemological groundings, the educational purposes, and the implementation requirements of these approaches (Liu & Ball, 2019, p. 81), labeled involvement, engagement, and solidarity. Teacher-community involvement, which is probably the most common approach in US K-12 education, consists of informational partnerships, focusing on one-way communication to provide families and communities with information about curriculum and policies. Teacher-community involvement positions students, families, and communities as the largely passive recipients of school-based expertise except in limited circumstances, such as the much-critiqued "flags and festivals" approach to multicultural education (Nieto, 2000). Teacher-community engagement includes instructional partnerships, aiming to involve families and communities in the instructional process through collaborative learning and consultation on decision-making, which brings communities into the schools, but still limits the role of community members and the sites of collaboration to the ultimate veto of school-based experts (Valenzuela, 1999). Teacher-community solidarity involves developing critical partnerships, emphasizing the engagement of families and communities in addressing broader social justice and equity issues within the educational system. Teacher-community solidarity thus attempts to shift education from traditional, school-centered systems of authority toward more inclusive and collaborative relationships that address not only academic but also social and systemic aspects of education.

Approaches such as those categorized by Zeichner et al. (2016) can also be applied to teacher education and have been termed "community-based teacher education" (Yuan, 2018; Zeichner, 2023). In Chap. 6 we provide an example of community-based teacher education; here we provide a brief summary of approaches various teacher educators have employed to bring teacher education programs into the community. One approach is to host community members as guest speakers in teacher education courses (Zeichner et al., 2016). This is parallel to the practice of hosting community members as guest speakers in K-12 classrooms, and thus runs the same risk of a "flags and festivals" reduction of a complex community into a small set of easily digested symbolic representations, providing prospective teachers with the mistaken impression of new-found expertise in community knowledge. However, as a foundation for deeper engagement with communities, providing a platform for community members to shape the initial orientation of prospective teachers to the community in which they will be placed can be more conducive to breaking down deficit views than if the same information were presented by a university-based expert.

Another approach to community-based teacher education that has been employed for some years is running teacher education courses in placement schools or community spaces (Darling-Hammond, 1994). In such a Professional Development School (PDS) approach, university-based teacher education supervisors are quartered in the placement schools where they are able to operate as part of the supervisor-mentor-prospective teacher triad on a daily basis and run one or more teacher education courses in situ. There are several advantages to this approach over limiting supervision and coursework to a university campus. For example, the primary instructor can more easily include school staff and community members as co-teachers in the course, and in-service teachers can also join the preservice teachers in their coursework, integrating professional development for the former into the preparation coursework of the latter.

Finally, there have been two other approaches to incorporating community members into the teacher education process. Zeichner et al. (2016) describe how members of a community-based grassroots organization (the Family Community Mentor Network) organized panel sessions, small-group discussions, and even short-term, one-credit courses designed and led by community members and addressing issues important to the community (pp. 281–282). The researchers reported success in shifting prospective teachers' attitudes toward the knowledge and resources that families and communities can bring to bear on their children's education (pp. 283–284), but also noted problems between the university-based program, the classroom mentor teachers and initial placement schools, and the community-based mentors. Some of these problems were institutional and hardly limited to this specific context.

However, other problems indicated a fundamental disconnect between the university base and the community base, including a lack of respect for community mentors by some of the university faculty and preservice teachers, and feelings or fear on the part of some prospective teachers, who felt personally attacked by community-based programming delving into racism and its manifestation in schools and schooling (p. 286). The study did not detail the demographics of either the preservice teacher population or the community in which the mentors were based, but we do note that, in our experience, these problems typically reflect a significant racial and cultural gap.

A more radical approach to developing and maintaining teacher-family solidarity is to empower communities to select and train the prospective teachers who will be working in that community. Pioneered by Zygmunt and colleagues at Ball State University and the African American community of Muncie, Indiana (Zygmunt et al., 2018a, b), this approach endeavors to integrate prospective teachers into the community through deep engagement with families and organizations. The process begins with a community panel that vets prospective teachers from a pool provided by the university teacher education program, selecting candidates for placement in their community. Selected prospective teachers then take part in extended homestay sessions, living with families in the community, participating in community activities, and conducting observations in the local school. Community members are also integrated into the teacher education curriculum and pedagogy, ensuring that coursework reflects the specific history, needs, and concerns of local families. After this homestay period, prospective students are placed in classrooms in the local school under the mentorship of an experienced teacher who is also a member of the community. The approach by Zygmunt et al. has shown significant success, but also points to potential pitfalls on both sides, primarily concerning the long-term maintenance of the program. For example, both university faculty and community members can experience burnout, making it imperative that both groups develop ways to maintain continuity even as specific personnel are replaced. Moreover, institutional and community politics can develop around a sense of membership in the program as an unearned privilege that needs to be shared regardless of commitment or qualifications, leading to interpersonal conflicts that need to be carefully navigated.

5.4   Conclusion

As we have seen, CRT was a useful lens for us to foreground the notions of race that we discovered in our earlier work on prospective teachers' reflections in online environments. Transforming a teacher education program's culture from one that may perpetuate racism to an anti-racist culture involves a comprehensive and sustained effort. Initiatives must begin with critical self-reflection and awareness, prompting faculty, administrators, and staff to examine their biases through training on cultural competence, implicit bias, and racism's impact on education. The curriculum needs a thorough review, ensuring inclusivity by incorporating anti-racist pedagogies and perspectives and authors from racialized communities. A commitment to racial equity in faculty and leadership is crucial, with active recruitment of individuals from minoritized backgrounds. Ongoing professional development programs should specifically address anti-racist practices, extending from preservice to in-service education. Community engagement becomes a priority, fostering partnerships with diverse communities and incorporating their perspectives and practices into program development. Anti-racist values should be embedded in policies, addressing incidents promptly and establishing clear reporting mechanisms. Cultivating inclusive learning environments involves proactive measures against microaggressions and conflict resolution resources. Evaluation metrics and accountability measures are essential, with continuous feedback loops and adjustments. Support networks for students, especially those from underrepresented backgrounds, should be developed. Lastly, an institutional commitment is necessary, with anti-racism principles integrated into the program's mission, vision, values, and resource allocation. This multifaceted approach emphasizes structural changes and cultural shifts, prioritizing diversity, equity, and inclusion at every level of the teacher education program. Our initial outcomes included nurturing habit of mind and habitual actions that would emerge from reflecting on what occurs in real-life teacher education programs in day-to-day settings. Over time, more equitable and inclusive materials are developed based on this shift of habits of mind and habitual actions. In turn, evidence-based approaches that are anti-racist take hold and create a new and vibrant culture for teacher education (Fig. 5.2).

Fostering anti-racist habits of mind among prospective teachers is a complex and intentional process that encompasses various strategies to shape both beliefs and actions. In our teacher education programs, we

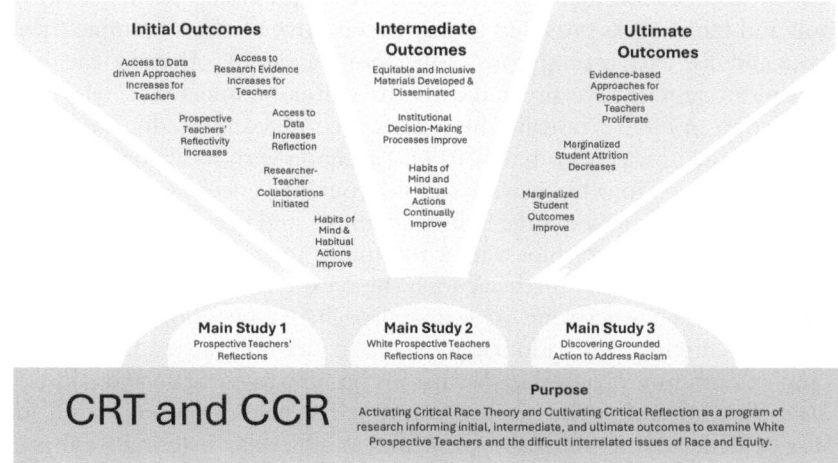

Fig. 5.2 Outcomes from cultivating critical reflection within a CRT framework

must prioritize critical pedagogy, infusing our curriculum with opportunities for students to critically examine societal structures, power dynamics, and historical injustices. Diverse perspectives are integral, and we must ensure that our curricula includes a rich tapestry of authors, voices, and experiences, challenging traditional narratives and promoting critical thinking on race and racism. This must involve using Critical Race Theory and Cultivating Critical Reflection. Our approach extends beyond the classroom, incorporating experiential learning opportunities such as field experiences and community engagement. These experiences enable prospective teachers to interact directly with diverse populations, fostering a deeper understanding of the realities faced by different communities. We emphasize critical reflection as a crucial component, encouraging students to analyze their experiences and confront their distorted assumptions. Modeling inclusive classroom patterns of action is central to our task. We must provide prospective and in-service teachers guidance on creating environments that are welcoming and affirming for all students, with an emphasis on strategies for differentiating instruction to meet diverse needs. Ongoing professional development opportunities are needed to focus on anti-racist pedagogies and strategies, empowering our prospective teachers to continuously deepen their understanding of racism and ways to combat it in educational settings.

Critical reflection and self-awareness are foundational elements, with tools and frameworks provided to help prospective teachers examine their biases and distorted assumptions. Anti-racist and equity-oriented teaching principles celebrate diversity and promote cultural competence, while an exploration of intersectionality highlights the interconnectedness of various social identities (Crenshaw, 2014). Engaging with local communities should be woven into teacher education programs, encouraging prospective teachers to understand the cultural contexts and needs of the students they will serve. Partnerships with community organizations focused on social justice and equity further enrich these experiences. Critical conversations form a cornerstone of our approach, encouraging prospective teachers to discuss real-world issues related to racism. Case studies present complex scenarios, prompting discussions on how to navigate and address issues of equity and justice in the classroom. Teacher education and a field must be dedicated to anti-racist principles at all levels, fostering a culture that values diversity, equity, and inclusion. Clear policies and practices must support these values, ensuring that our teacher education program not only imparts knowledge and skills but also cultivates a mindset that actively implement transformative actions to opposes racism in all its forms.

We have arrived at this through a long-term program of research grounded in the theory work on race and racism and education over a long period of time. Clearly, this is not done. It would be ironic if we were to be unreflective in our work about reflection. We have a long way to go. We must continue to support the work of research and theory building to continually refine the work of teacher education and to nurture the emergence of anti-racist habits of mind and patterns of acting and resist toxicity even when it appears among ourselves. In the next chapter, we will continue to explore cultivating critical reflection while providing a brief survey of possible ways in which to restructure teacher education to transform habits of mind and patterns of acting concerning race and racism among White preservice teachers.

REFERENCES

Alexander, M. (2012). *The new Jim Crow: Mass incarceration in the age of color-blindness*. The New Press.

Alim, H. S., & Paris, D. (2017). What is culturally sustaining pedagogy and why does it matter? In D. Paris & H. S. Alim (Eds.), *Culturally sustaining pedagogies: Teaching and Learning for Justice in a changing world* (pp. 1–23). Teachers College Press.

Annamma, S. A. (2017). *The pedagogy of pathologization: Dis/abled girls of color in the school-prison nexus.* Routledge.

Aronson, B., & Meyers, L. (2020). Critical race theory and the teacher education curriculum: Challenging understandings of racism, whiteness, and white supremacy. *Whiteness and Education, 7*(1), 32–57.

Basile, V., York, A., & Black, R. (2022). Who Is the one being disrespectful? Understanding and deconstructing the criminalization of elementary school boys of color. *Urban Education, 57*(9), 1592–1620.

Bryan, N. (2017). White teachers' role in sustaining the school-to-prison pipeline: Recommendations for teacher education. *The Urban Review, 49*(2), 326–345.

Chen, D. A., Lord, S. M., Mejia, J. A., & Hoople, G. D. (2021). A critical reflection on the challenges of implementing culturally sustaining pedagogy. *IEEE Frontiers in Education Conference (FIE), 2021*, 1–5.

Cochran-Smith, M., & Villegas, A. M. (2015). Studying teacher preparation: The questions that drive research. *European Educational Research Journal, 14*(5), 379–394.

Crenshaw, K. (2014). *On intersectionality.* NEW Press.

Darling-Hammond, L. (Ed.). (1994). *Professional development schools: Schools for developing a profession.* Teachers College Press.

DiAngelo, R. (2018). *White fragility: Why it's so hard for White people to talk about racism.* Beacon Press.

Estrada, F., & Matthews, G. (2016). Perceived culpability in critical multicultural education: Understanding and responding to race informed guilt and shame to further learning outcomes among White American college students. *International Journal of Teaching and Learning in Higher Education, 28*(3), 314–325.

Evans-Winters, V. E., & Twyman Hoff, P. (2011). The aesthetics of white racism in pre-service teacher education: A critical race theory perspective. *Race Ethnicity and Education, 14*(4), 461–479.

Gadd, R. (2023). 'You can say that they were being racist': Confronting white comfort in anti-racist teacher education. *Whiteness and Education, 8*(2), 159–176.

Glaser, B. (1978). *Theoretical sensitivity: Advances in the methodology of grounded theory.* Sociology Press.

Glaser, B. (1998). *Doing grounded theory: Issues and discussions.* Sociology Press.

Glaser, B. G., & Strauss, A. L. (1967). *The discovery of Grounded Theory: Strategies for qualitative research.* Aldine.

Graue, E. (2005). Theorizing and describing preservice teachers' images of families and schooling. *Teachers College Record, 107*(1), 157–185.

Greenman, N. P., & Kimmel, E. B. (1995). The road to multicultural education: Potholes of resistance. *Journal of Teacher Education, 46*(5), 360–368.

Harvey, J. E. (2023). Teaching, power, and the belief in school meritocracy. Ph.D. dissertation, Fordham University.

Hollins, E. R. (2019). *Teaching to transform urban schools and communities: Powerful pedagogy in practice*. Routledge.

Howard, T. C. (2010). *Why race and culture matter in schools: Closing the achievement gap in America's classrooms*. Teachers College Press.

Joyner, M. (2024). *Preparing anti-racist teachers: A case study of preservice teachers' perceptions of racism and program coherence in equity-centered teacher preparation*. (Publication No. 5127) [Doctoral Dissertation, University of Nevada, Las Vegas]. https://digitalscholarship.unlv.edu/thesesdissertations/5127

Kendi, I. X. (2019). *How to be an antiracist*. One World.

Klein, E. (2020). *Why we're polarized*. Avid Reader Press.

Ladson-Billings, G. (1995). Toward a theory of culturally relevant pedagogy. *American Educational Research Journal, 32*(3), 465–491.

Ladson-Billings, G. (2009). *The dreamkeepers: Successful teachers of African American children* (2nd ed.). John Wiley & Sons.

LaDuke, A. E. (2009). Resistance and renegotiation: Preservice teacher interactions with and reactions to multicultural education course content. *Multicultural Education, 16*(3), 37–44.

Lipsitz, G. (1995). The possessive investment in whiteness: Racialized social democracy and the "White" problem in American studies. *American Quarterly, 47*(3), 369–387.

Liu, K. (2011). Enhancing prospective teachers' critical reflection in the ePortfolio environment. Ph.D. dissertation, University of Wisconsin-Madison.

Liu, K. (2017). Creating a dialogic space for prospective teacher critical reflection and transformative learning. *Reflective Practice: International and Multidisciplinary Perspectives, 18*(6), 805-820.

Liu, K. (2020). *Critical reflection for transformative learning: Understanding ePortfolios in teacher education*. Springer.

Liu, K., & Ball, A. (2019). Critical reflection and generativity: Toward a framework of transformative teacher education for diverse learners. *Review of Research in Education, 43*(1), 68–105.

Liu, K., Miller, R., & Ball, A. F. (2023). Teacher education for diverse learners. In R. J. Tierney, F. Rizvi, & K. Erkican (Eds.), *International encyclopedia of education, vol. 5* (pp. 356–367). Elsevier.

Lortie, D. (1975). *Schoolteacher: A sociological study*. University of Chicago Press.

Love, B. (2019). *We want to do more than survive: Abolitionist teaching and the pursuit of educational freedom*. Beacon Press.

Martell, C. C., Harris, L. M., Lee, J., Chalmers, J. P., & Carmichael, J. (2024). Silent covenants and structural barriers: State standards committees and the maintenance of race-evasive social studies standards. *AERA Open, 10*. https://doi.org/10.1177/23328584241265303

Matias, C. E., & Mackey, J. (2016). Breakin'down whiteness in antiracist teaching: Introducing critical whiteness pedagogy. *The Urban Review, 48*(1), 32–50.

Matias, C. E., Montoya, R., & Nishi, N. W. M. (2016). Blocking CRT: How the emotionality of whiteness blocks CRT in urban teacher education. *Educational Studies, 52*(1), 1–19.

McKamey, P. (2020). What anti-racist teachers do differently: They view the success of Black students as central to the success of their own teaching. *The Atlantic,* June 17, 2020. Retrieved June 24, 2020, from https://www.theatlantic.com/education/archive/2020/06/how-be-anti-racist-teacher/613138/

Mildred, J., & Zúñiga, X. (2004). Working with resistance to diversity issues in the classroom: Lessons from teacher training and multicultural education. *Smith College Studies in Social Work, 74*(2), 359–375.

Miller, R., Liu, K., & Ball, A. (2020). Critical counter-narrative as transformative methodology for educational equity. *Review of Research in Education, 44*(1), 269–300.

Milner, H. R. (2010). *Start where you are but don't stay there: Understanding diversity, opportunity gaps, and teaching in today's classrooms.* Harvard Education Press.

Milner, H. R. (2012). But what is urban education? *Urban Education, 47*(3), 556–561.

Milner, H. R. (2021). *Start where you are but don't stay there: Understanding diversity, opportunity gaps, and teaching in today's classrooms* (2nd ed.). Harvard Education Press.

Milner, H. R. (2023). *The race card: Leading the fight for truth in America's schools.* Corwin.

Muhammad, G. (2023). *Unearthing Joy: A guide to culturally and historically responsive curriculum and instruction.* Scholastic.

Murrell, P. (2000). Community teachers: A conceptual framework for preparing exemplary urban teachers. *Journal of Negro Education, 69,* 338–348.

Nieto, S. (2000). *Affirming diversity: The sociopolitical context of multicultural education.* Longman.

Oakes, J., Franke, M. L., Quartz, K. H., & Rogers, J. (2002). Research for high-quality urban teaching: Defining it, developing it, assessing it. *Journal of Teacher Education, 53*(3), 228–234.

Oamek, K. (2024). White preservice teachers and antiracist practice: Enabling trajectories of learning and identity in teacher preparation. *Action in Teacher Education, 46*(1), 56–74.

Paris, D. (2012). Culturally sustaining pedagogy: A needed change in stance, terminology, and practice. *Educational Researcher, 41*(3), 93–97.

Shim, J. M. (2018). Working through resistance to resistance in anti-racist teacher education. *Journal of Philosophy of Education, 52*(2), 262–283.

Simmons, O., & Gregory, T. A. (2003). Grounded action: Achieving optimal and sustainable change. *FQS, 4*(3.27) https://www.qualitative-research.net/index.php/fqs/article/view/677/1464

Simmons, O. E. (2022). *Experiencing grounded theory: A comprehensive guide to learning, doing, mentoring, teaching, and applying grounded theory.* BrownWalker Press.

Skiba, R. J., Arredondo, M. I., & Williams, N. T. (2014). More than a metaphor: The contribution of exclusionary discipline to a school-to- prison pipeline. *Equity & Excellence in Education, 47*(4), 546–564.

Sleeter, C. (1995). *Multicultural education, critical pedagogy, and the politics of difference.* State University of New York Press.

St. Denis, V., & Schick, C. (2003). What makes anti-racist pedagogy in teacher education difficult? Three popular ideological assumptions. *Alberta Journal of Educational Research, 49*(1).

Stovall, D. O. (2016). *Born out of struggle: Critical race theory, school creation, and the politics of interruption.* State University of New York Press.

Tatum, B. D. (2017). *Why are all the Black kids sitting together in the cafeteria? And other conversations about race.* Basic Books.

Thomas, M. K., & Liu, K. (2012). The performance of reflection: A grounded analysis of prospective teachers' ePortfolios. *Journal of Technology and Teacher Education, 20*(3), 305–330.

Valenzuela, A. (1999). *Subtractive schooling: U.S.-Mexican youth and the politics of caring.* State University of New York Press.

Yuan, H. (2018). Preparing teachers for diversity: A literature review and implications from community-based teacher education. *Higher Education Studies, 8*(1), 9–17.

Zeichner, K., Bowman, M., Guillen, L., & Napolitan, K. (2016). Engaging and working in solidarity with local communities in preparing teachers of their children. *Journal of Teacher Education, 67*(4), 277–290.

Zeichner, K., & Payne, K. (2013). Democratizing knowledge in urban teacher education. In J. Noel (Ed.), *Moving teacher education into urban schools and communities* (pp. 3–19). Routledge.

Zeichner, K. M. (2023). *Communities: Keywords in teacher education.* Bloomsbury.

Zygmunt, E., Cipollone, K., Clark, P., & Tancock, S. (2018a). Community-engaged teacher preparation. In *Oxford research encyclopedia of education.* Oxford University Press.

Zygmunt, E., Cipollone, K., Tancock, S., Clausen, J., Clark, P., & Mucherah, W. (2018b). Loving out loud: Community mentors, teacher candidates, and transformational learning through a pedagogy of care and connection. *Journal of Teacher Education, 69*(2), 127–139.

CHAPTER 6

Cultivating Critical Reflection for Transformative Learning in the Context of Race

6.1 Returning to the Transformative Teacher Education Framework

As we embarked on this journey, we went about constructing this book using a theoretical framework encompassing three elements: (1) Critical Race Theory (CRT); (2) culturally relevant and sustaining community-based teacher education; and (3) critical reflection and generative change for transformative action. Following Liu et al., (2023), we use the metaphor of travel in which the destination is the "transformation of the educational system to affect educational equity" (p. 371). As elaborated in Chap. 2, for this journey, CRT provides the roadmap to equity, culturally relevant and sustaining community-based teacher education provides the vehicle, and the engine is powered by critical reflection and generative change for transformative action (See Fig. 6.1). In this chapter, we first explain the role of community-based teacher education as a powerful praxis for the framework, explaining the process through which we develop prospective teachers' ability to recognize, elicit, and in some cases develop counter-narratives to serve as the core of their critical reflection and guide their transformative action. We then describe how the acts of counter-narrative are placed in the community through community-based teacher education activities. We conclude the chapter with some examples of classroom and placement activities that scaffold the stages of critical reflection for transformative action.

K. Liu et al., *Preparing White Teachers for Anti-Racist Education*, https://doi.org/10.1007/978-3-031-73534-9_6

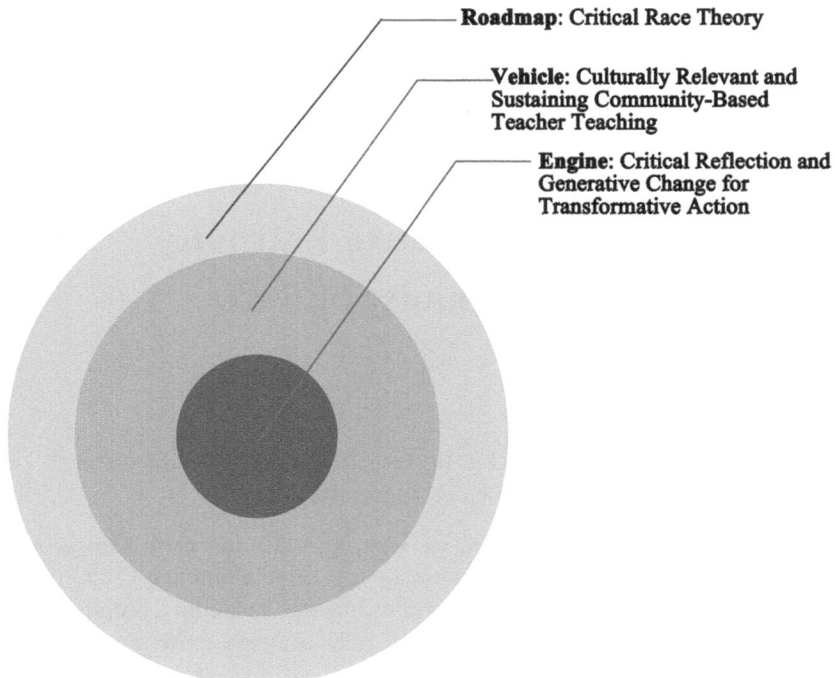

Roadmap: Critical Race Theory

Vehicle: Culturally Relevant and
Sustaining Community-Based
Teacher Teaching

Engine: Critical Reflection and
Generative Change for
Transformative Action

Fig. 6.1   Transformative teacher education for anti-racist education

6.2   IMPLEMENTING COMMUNITY-BASED
TEACHER EDUCATION

Building on the previous chapters of this book, we propose developing a transformative anti-racist teacher education community that includes mentor teachers and other supporting personnel in schools, university-based teacher educators, parents, community members, and prospective teachers. In such a community, prospective teachers should be considered as active participants and change agents, bringing their unique perspectives, struggles, voices, and wisdom to the co-construction of teacher education knowledge and practice. However, uniting the four parties together by itself will not automatically make it a transformative community. The habits of mind and patterns of acting of the White prospective teachers described in the previous chapters did not demonstrate transformative learning and a move toward anti-racist praxis—yet they were, to some extent, part of a community, mentored and supervised by the mentor teachers and university supervisors. Some of them included parents and community members in their teaching as well. Bringing together the four groups thus presents both promise and challenge. The promise is clear; the challenge is how to fulfill that promise. In order to overcome these challenges, we employ the theoretical framework discussed in Chap. 2— CRT, culturally relevant and sustaining pedagogies, community-based teacher education, and critical reflection and generative change for transformative action—focused on the goal of social justice and educational equity, to unite the four parties in creating a transformative, anti-racist teacher education community (Fig. 6.2).

As described in Chap. 5, setting teacher education within communities rather than segregating the programs and participants within a university is vital to give White prospective teachers opportunities to reflect upon

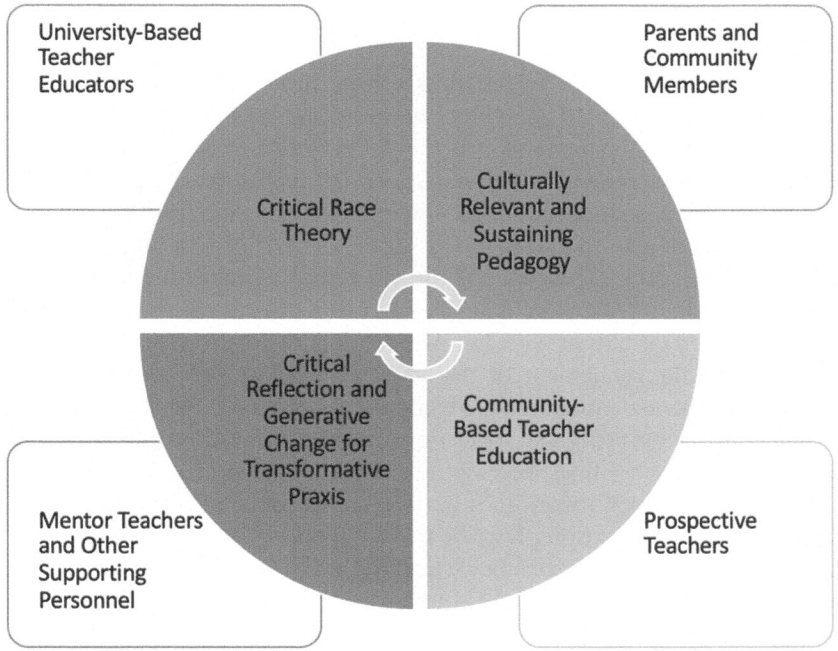

Fig. 6.2 Anti-racist transformative teacher education community

and reimagine their relationships with students and families from minoritized communities. Intensive engagement with community members in both formal and informal settings can help White prospective teachers recognize and value their students' community funds of knowledge and rebalance the power relations between school and community too often reinscribed by university-centric, technically focused teacher education programs. This engagement must be implemented in nuanced ways so as to make space for agency on the part of community members in shaping curriculum, content, and pedagogy. It is important to note that the community needs to be formed with intentionality, comprising members who are dedicated to the goals of transforming schooling through anti-racist teaching. The end of Chap. 5 discussed a few approaches teacher educators have employed to bring teacher education programs into the community—community-based teacher education.

6.3   Scaffolding Critical Reflection and Generativity for Transformative Anti-racist Teaching

Bearing in mind the life experiences prospective teachers bring to their careers, Katrina designed a series of classroom and field placement activities that employed a framework of critical reflection for transformative learning (Liu, 2020) in a broadly collaborative, community-oriented approach to guide systematic instruction in teaching minoritized students. These activities were developed and refined in a variety of teacher education courses, culminating in multiple offerings of an elementary general methods course for students in an Alternate Route to Licensure program at Desert View University Liu co-taught with Dr. Arnetha Ball, who also contributed significantly to the refinement of the activities. Within each step of critical reflection, Katrina integrated pedagogical tools to facilitate prospective teachers' thinking processes, focusing particularly on racism and racialized experiences in schooling, developing collaboration and community, and aiming toward transformation of both habits of mind and patterns of acting. The following sections describe these activities in terms of the stages of critical reflection for transformative learning and in terms of the goals articulated throughout this book. Although we encourage other teacher educators to use these projects in order to scaffold critical reflection and generative change, we do not provide tools to assess the reflections of the prospective teachers. As we have argued throughout this book, authentic critical reflection and the potential for transformation cannot survive a regime of surveillance, checklists, and standardized rubrics, which encourage prospective teachers in pursuit of performativity to avoid opportunities for critical reflection in favor of the depiction of mastery. Instead, dialogic, collaborative reflection among peers, when undertaken in a community-based context and a non-evaluative environment, can stimulate authentic critical reflection as well as moves toward transformative action. In keeping with the overall model for this book, all processes are firmly grounded in the principles of CRT and should be undertaken in the specific context of real communities. In other words, although we follow a general sequence, everything in this chapter should be tailored to the prospective teachers, teacher education programs, schools, school systems, and local communities in which teacher education actually occurs. The pedagogical tools designed for the course follow the sequence of critical reflection and generative change for transformative learning:

1. Stimulate initial self-reflection through assumption analysis and contextual awareness;
2. Begin to envision other ways of being and doing through imaginative speculation and reflective skepticism; and
3. Develop transformative solutions based on the previous stages, gain knowledge and skills from parents and local community members to implement the solutions, pilot them, and then reflect again on the impact of those actions on teachers, students, and the community to generate new knowledge for further transformation.

6.4   Stimulate Self-Reflection Through Assumption Analysis and Contextual Awareness

Self-reflection begins at the first two stages of critical reflection and generative change, Assumption Analysis and Contextual Awareness that can activate metacognitive awareness and ideological becoming (Ball, 2009; Miller et al., 2020). In these stages, prospective teachers collaboratively reflect on their lived experiences of schools and schooling through shared dialog scaffolded with critical perspectives on race and factors that intersect with race. The primary goal is to help them identify the assumptions about schooling and society that underlie the ideas, beliefs, values, and actions that they (and others) take for granted, and then measure the accuracy and validity of these assumptions against lived experiences. This process also helps prospective teachers realize that their assumptions are socially and personally created in the specific historical and cultural context in which they live. Thus at this stage prospective teachers reflect on their positionality and lived experiences in schooling and society. Critical counter-narrative is used throughout the process to create a space for prospective teachers of and parents and members from minoritized communities to share their lieved experiences countering the norms of schooling and the stereotypes about minoritized students and their communities. The process begins with three pedagogical tools to help prospective teachers understand themselves as individuals and teachers first in terms of self-conception (the *Museum of Me* project), and then in terms of their experiences with schooling and broader society (the *Privilege Race* and *Coding Social Networks* projects). Prospective teachers then pivot toward their placement school and community by using public sources to describe the assets available in the community to support their school and students (the *Mapping Community Assets* project). With this abstract picture of community assets, prospective teachers then engage directly with community members to understand how in-service teachers, administrators, students, parents, and other community members see themselves and the processes of schooling (the *Community Panel* project).

6.4.1   *Museum of Me*

Museum of Me was an activity aimed at getting prospective teachers to tell stories about themselves, and then place those stories in a critical relation to schools and schooling. This activity was modified from one developed by Dr. Edric Johnson, Professor of Curriculum and Instruction at the University of Wisconsin-Whitewater and a specialist in social studies and arts integration. Richard also developed electronic media variants of this project for an online course on teaching music in higher education that involved slide decks and recorded pecha-kucha presentations. However, whether performed in-person or online, the general procedure remained the same: prospective teachers were instructed to bring six to eight artifacts they feel represent themselves, choosing items to help them to tell a story addressing the following aspects of their life story:

1. Who am I? What are my different identities?
2. What was my previous life and education like?
3. How did my previous experiences shape who I am today?
4. What are my strengths and family/community assets? What kind of teacher do I want to be in the future?

Prospective teachers were guided to include artifacts that reveal something about their intersectinoal identities, their history and culture, their likes, career, character traits, etc. Here are some examples of artifacts (This is not a complete list—creativity is desirable):

1. Favorite quote(s), food, song(s), sports team, holidays, maps, hobbies, books, pets—(just a photo please)
2. Location of where you live—or grew up (e.g., a map)
3. Academic interests
4. Examples of work

In face-to-face classes, participants created one card for each artifact that briefly described it. In Richard's online version, prospective teachers provided brief captions or voiceover annotations. During class, prospective teachers formed small groups of three to four members, taking turns sharing their stories. After sharing, each prospective teacher created an exhibit using their artifacts and the description cards; the class then circulated around the room, visiting each other's exhibit. At the end of the exhibition, prospective teachers wrote stories about themselves using the four questions above as prompts, adding one question that promoted them to reflect on what they learned about themselves that they never thought before.

Over time, as we engaged in this activity with multiple cohorts of prospective teachers, certain patterns became evident. First, all prospective teachers included artifacts linked to their identities as individuals, such as a baseball and a coach's whistle, photos of a favorite hike, or a map of their hometown. However, prospective teachers from minoritized communities also tended to include artifacts linked to their non-White identities—a Mexican flag, a Hawai'ian *lei*, pictures of a hotpot for Chinese New Year. White prospective teachers, on the other hand, generally did not include artifacts linked to group identity beyond sports or religious activities. For example, a student who is half Colombian and half Filipino shared artifacts of a Colombian flag and a magnet she bought when she visited the Philippines. In her artifacts cards, this student wrote:

I am half Colombian so this next artifact means a lot to me, the Colombian flag. This country means a lot to me. My mother didn't speak much English when she came to the U.S. and hearing and watching her speak near perfect English now is so admirable. I can understand and I can speak Spanish but mostly because I made sure of it (I studied it in school so as to not lose that part of my heritage) and minored in Spanish during my undergraduate years. My other half is Filipino, my dad was born in the Philippines and I grew up with that side of the family a lot more. This next artifact is a magnet I got when I went to visit [the Philippines] for the first and only time. I don't speak the language and I can only understand it in context of the situation.

Second, although most prospective teachers included artifacts representing their chosen career in teaching, only those with prior experience in the classroom as teachers or teacher aides used something specifically from their experience, such as a school staff name badge or appreciation cards from their students. Prospective teachers whose sole experience in the classroom was as a student tended to represent teachers with generic images, such as a cartoon drawing of a one-room schoolhouse or clipart of someone writing on a chalkboard.

Because of the dialogic nature of the activity, though, with participants commenting and questioning each other's exhibits, these differences between White and non-White, experienced and inexperienced participants enabled all prospective teachers to begin understanding themselves as occupying specific subject positions within schooling and society, as individuals with personal, family, and community histories, and as people standing at the nexus of educational generations, students and teachers at the same time. Through the remainder of the teacher education program, they returned to their museums as well as those of their fellow classmates, looking for insight into their assumptions and conceptions of schools, schooling, students, and communities, and drawing strength from their own community funds of knowledge in taking the first steps toward becoming critically reflective teachers. The student we quoted earlier in this section reflected after the Museum of Me activity that this activity encouraged her to think about herself and her backgrounds, which she planned to implement in her future teaching:

> I really enjoyed thinking and reflecting on these special artifacts in my home because as we discussed in class, these artifacts were just a part of life and not something we necessarily think about often. I hope to bring an activity similar to this (or even exactly like this) to my future classroom so we can all share our stories. Being able to speak about our culture and what makes us who we are is what will

bond us together as a class and as a community. Finding similarities and differences can help alleviate the thought that we are alone and that no one understands. I hope to have my class present to the rest of the class something about themselves but also to share in smaller groups as we did because it can be intimidating to explain to a whole room who you are and why. I want my class to feel comfortable, so sharing in a smaller group and having them find similarities will be a fun and interactive activity.

6.4.2 The Privilege Race

The *Privilege Race* activity was inspired by Peggy McIntosh's 1989 article on White privilege as an "invisible knapsack." In this article she describes some of the unearned privileges she identified as stemming from the social status given to her skin color that were not shared by her Black colleagues. The article, along with a companion piece (McIntosh, 2010) provides some ways to make use of such lists as part of consciousness-raising activities. McIntosh's list activity has been adapted numerous times over the past few decades. Katrina has adapted it each semester for the specific situation of the program participants and the schools in which they were placed. Prospective teachers were asked to stand up in a row. They were then shown a series of statements representing aspects of a person's upbringing, their family's intersectional identities, and their own life experiences, phrased (as McIntosh, 1989 and 2010 suggests) in terms of the privileges associated in the United States with White, middle-class life, such as "I never worried about the utilities shutting off," "I never went short of food," "I was never followed by a security guard while shopping." After each statement, prospective teachers were asked to take one step forward if the statement was true to their experience; if not, they were asked to take one step backward. At the end of the activity, participants were asked to look at who had taken many steps forward, and who had not taken any, or only taken a few. General discussion followed as all participants discussed their experiences with privilege and the idea that there is a quality of invisibility to privilege.

In Katrina's experience, participants in the Privilege Race typically observed that a few White prospective teachers moved far ahead, agreeing with virtually every statement, while a significant percentage of prospective teachers of color were left behind. For example, in one cohort, Jevon, an African American male, only moved forward on two statements: "I graduated from high school" and "I graduated from college." After this was pointed out, a heated discussion took place about the implications of the Privilege Race for assumptions about opportunity and success in life and education. Jevon first shared his story that he was always considered as a "troublemaker" at school and had the experience of being followed by security guards in stores all the time. Jevon then disclosed that he was jailed for six months for a crime that he never committed, and on release was not even charged. Nevertheless, Jevon continued,

> During this privilege race, every time I was not able to move forward reminded me simultaneously of my painful past and my proud present. Unlike what some of my teachers told me before, I'm not less intelligent; I'm not less hardworking. I graduated from high school. I graduated from college, and I'm here today and I'm here to support kids like me.

The Privilege Race, and especially counter-narratives like that relayed by Jevon, helped the entire class question the taken-for-granted assumptions that all students have the same opportunity, that lack of success means lack of interest or effort on their part, and that invisible or not, White privilege is not a myth. One White prospective teacher responded in an interview that

> Jevon's story helped me to understand that people don't really have the same opportunity. It's sad to see how the structure of the country sets people down. Like Jevon, he didn't do anything wrong, but he was put in jail and he was left far behind in the privilege race.

A White prospective teacher shared in class her story of privilege:

> I had the privilege of getting into GATE [Gifted and Talented Education]. My dad is a lawyer and when I was in elementary school, he fought to get me in GATE. He learned that I could test in not through the school so he lined up for hours to register for the test for me. I got into GATE. When I became a parent, I wanted my children to be in GATE so we moved specifically to a school for that purpose. Now the school where I teach is located in a non-White community and when I mentioned GATE to parents, most of them did not know anything about it.

This student's story about her experiences in GATE inspired Katrina to share data on GATE access disparity and inequity in the local district. The Privilege Race activity also helped prospective teachers of color realize that their personal experiences did not stand alone; sharing their stories with each other validated their experiences and helped situate them in the larger social, political, cultural, and historical context of schooling and society, providing them the opportunity to synthesize a range of disparate experiences into a coherent resource for imagining transformation.

However, it is important to note that White prospective teachers often responded to the Privilege Race, and the counter-narratives that emerged from it, with resistance and denial. For example, after one of the cohorts completed the exercise, a White male prospective teacher responded with anger, first acknowledging that they experienced privilege but then undercutting that statement by proclaiming "I'm privileged but I'm not lazy or bad. I worked for what I got." Another White prospective teacher, someone from a relatively poor family background who had entered the military out of high school, insisted that "talking about institutional racism denies the experiences of White people like me who struggle financially." This White resistance has been commonly noted to take various forms in research on multicultural teacher education (Bruna, 2005; Dunn et al., 2014; Evans-Winter & Hines, 2019; Gonsalves, 2008; LaDuke, 2009). The resistance may take forms such as outright denial, personal affront, and most strongly, complete silence. We have also identified patterns in prospective teachers' reflection artifacts, such as pledging commitment, that also can function as resistance to the Privilege Race activity, deflecting attention from the prospective teacher's own subject position by focusing on their promises for an undefined future.

All of these acts of resistance to the very notion of White privilege at times became flash points for disagreement within the classroom, leading to discomfort and, in some cases, one or more White prospective teachers demonstrating anger. It is vital, however, that teacher educators not avoid such moments of discomfort while teaching about white privilege. Teacher educators need to help White prospective teachers recognize the unearned privileges provided to them and how these privileges directly deprive individuals of color equal rights and opportunities (McIntosh, 2010; Milner, 2010, 2023). In responding to resistance such as the White student who insisted that they experienced poverty, teacher educators can point out that recognizing white privilege does not mean that White individuals never experience challenges; instead, it means White individuals as a group are much less likely to suffer from an inequitable distribution of the resources that are fundamental for success (Crenshaw et al., 1996). Teacher educators need to help White prospective teachers experience discomfort regarding white privilege, and then interrogate their reasons for taking personal offense, an inherently privileged response that prioritizes white feelings and emotions above intergenerational racial injustice and oppression experienced by individuals of color (Matias, 2018). Working through White discomfort by having those white feelings and tears deconstructed and decentered is an important element in growing as an antiracist teacher (Matias, 2018). At the same time, prospective teachers from minoritized communities need to see their own experiences and viewpoints centered in the classroom, and be supported in the face of White denial. This support and centering is key to retaining non-White prospective teachers in the program and the profession, a task that is vital to increasing the diversity of the teacher corps as a whole, in addition to its importance to individual teachers' career success.

6.4.3   Coding Social Networks

The first two activities described above, Museum of Me and the Privilege Race, helped prospective teachers begin to see how their subject position in schooling and society linked to their personal history and identity. The next step was for prospective teachers to use that knowledge of their subject position to turn their gaze toward larger schooling and society. Prospective teachers were first given a set of readings providing the ethnic and racial breakdown of student achievement statistics as well as a similar demographic breakdown of high-status, highly paid professions in the United States. After some discussion on these statistics, a key inspiration for the activity was the article by Gloria Ladson-Billings, *From the achievement gap to the education debt* (Ladson-Billings, 2006). This pivotal work reframed the understanding of differences in K-12 student achievement linked to race and class away from the idea that underperformance by members of minoritized groups is a matter of psychological, social, and cultural deficits in the students, their families, and their communities. Rather, Ladson-Billings argued that the achievement gap results from deficits in equity, especially educational equity but also broader social and political equity. Ladson-Billings explains that there is an education debt owed to minoritized groups resulting from segregation, deliberate underfunding of non-White students, schools, and teachers, and persistent discrimination against non-White students and families across society as well as in schools.

With this reading in mind, prospective teachers were challenged to become aware of the generations of education debt that perpetuate the achievement gap experienced by minoritized students and teachers. An important element in developing this awareness was for prospective teachers to code the characteristics of their own social network, and then use the results for comparison and analysis in class. In this exercise, prospective teachers were given a list of social roles and professions that they engaged with throughout their lives such as with their first-grade teachers, third-grade teachers, pediatricians, dentists, high school principals, janitors in middle school, high school counselors, plumbers, best friends in elementary school, and so forth. Then, they were given instruction to guide the network coding:

1. Briefly describe your racial, ethnic, linguistic, and cultural backgrounds; analyze the kind of neighborhood you grew up in: Where is it? What kind of diversity does it have?
2. Code the racial, ethnic, linguistic, and cultural backgrounds of the people in the list based on your observation.
3. Make a bar chart to represent your findings.
4. Based on your findings, what are your thoughts about your social network in terms of diversity and privilege?

Once the coding was complete, prospective teachers shared their coded networks, findings, and thoughts with each other.

Reading the statistical reports of the education debt (Ladson-Billings, 2006) and its impact on student learning outcomes through literature gave prospective teachers an abstract sense of the segregation and discrimination meted out to members of minoritized communities; coding and sharing their own social networks made those statistics come alive. White prospective teachers could read the statistic that 91% of the members of the average White person's social network are also White (Cox et al., 2016) without reflecting on their own position in this statistical reality. The network exercise forced them to link their identities and their positions in schooling and society directly to the identities and positions of the people around them. Sharing findings and thoughts were central to this process, as so much of the Whiteness of organizations and professions was truly invisible not only to White prospective teachers but to prospective teachers of color as well. For example, a Latina prospective teacher, who grew up in a predominantly Latinx community, shared that she thought her networks would be representing her community, but she was shocked after she did the coding: The only other Latinx people in her network were the middle school janitor, her best friend in elementary school, the mail carrier, and yard workers. Everyone else who held more privileged positions in her network was White, even though her community was predominantly Latinx. Another Latinx prospective teacher grew up in a relatively White community, yet his story was very similar. There were only four non-White people in his network, a 6th grade female African American teacher, his best friend in elementary school (Black), an African American professor, and a Mexican plumber.

Sharing and collaboratively reflecting on each other's social networks helped prospective teachers address one of the core questions posed by CRT in general, and Critical Whiteness in particular: How does privilege exist in our society? Prospective teachers expressed that the people who do the janitor's job, people who clean yards, were not less intelligent or less hardworking. What they lacked were opportunities for them to achieve their greatest potential. This activity helped prospective teachers of color to see the social reality of privilege and inequity. It further helped them challenge the notion of meritocracy. They had never made a connection between the racial/ethnic distribution among the people they interacted with and the inequities in our society, and noted the high percentage of White people holding more privileged positions in both networks regardless of the racial/ethnic mix of their community.

These activities led to an important stage of generative change (Ball, 2009), "awakening"—a metacognitive process that enables prospective teachers to start situating personal experiences in the larger society: "I'm in this situation due to societal problems" (Miller et al., 2020, p. 290). For some prospective teachers such as Jevon, these activities also activated their "ideological becoming," finding agency to change the situation through their deliberate actions as teachers (Ball, 2009; Miller et al., 2021).

6.5   Pivoting Toward School and Community

So far in the process, the critical reflection and generativity activities focused on helping prospective teachers develop awareness of their subject position in schooling and society with an emphasis on their historical path to their current career choice as well as their ideological becoming as teachers. With the next two projects, prospective teachers began to build an understanding of the school and community in which they were placed.

The first activity, Mapping Community Assets, was designed to familiarize prospective students with some of the broad characteristics of the school and community, including demographics, local social and cultural features, and resources that could combine to form a pool of community funds of knowledge for instruction in the school. Once the prospective teachers completed that assignment, Liu organized panel sessions in placement schools to provide community members the opportunity to directly address prospective teachers regarding their experiences, and those of their children, in schooling and society. The aim of these two activities was to push back against the deficit model of minoritized students and their communities and afford students and families a forum to speak up for themselves, asserting agency rather than being cast as passive recipients of (White) expertise. Attacking both the deficit model of minoritized students and the "White savior" vision of the prospective teachers with real data and real community voices is a vital step in developing anti-racist approaches to education.

6.6   MAPPING COMMUNITY ASSETS

Prospective teachers were directed to collect information on the community served by their placement school via publicly available sources on city, district, school, and/or lived experiences in the community. This information included items such as reports from the school district, news stories, and personal stories. Prompts for this collection (samples shown in Table 6.1) were deliberately constructed to be general and open ended. They were intended to encourage prospective teachers to dig into the specific features of the community, and not just fill out a simple checklist that would not accurately reflect the lives of the students and their families, and the ways in which they and their placement school could engage with the community. The guiding question was "What can you learn from and about the community that you can integrate into your teaching?"

The results prospective teachers reported regarding their research on city, district, and school were rather general. This was expected as they could not incorporate the voices from the community, and the choice of resources that generally reflect the prospective teachers' own sense of what was important. For example, one White prospective teacher provided basic city and school demographics (race, gender, income level), and centered their placement school within a community of city resources (parks, recreational facilities, service centers) and churches—but did not explore

Table 6.1   Prompts for prospective teachers' community knowledge development

Information category	Example
Population	City, district, and school size
Demographics	City, district, and school:
	Racial/ethnic/gender breakdown
	Income levels
	Parent education levels
	School:
	Percentage free/reduced lunch
	Attendance area
	Transportation methods
	After-school programs
Community Resources	Community organizations and centers
	Grocery stores and markets
	Employment opportunities
	Medical services
	Religious institutions
	Community activities (sports, arts, social)
	Festivals and events
Summarize Community Strengths	Community food production
	Neighborhood watch organization
	Neighborhood rotating credit organization
	Cooperative childcare organization
	Shared language and cultural background
	Close ties to school

service organizations, community events, grocery stores, or employment opportunities. Moreover, in response to the question about community strengths, the same White prospective teacher provided only a sentence fragment, "diverse cultures that make up the community around [School Name]." The only truly local detail was the observation that many families kept chickens in their backyards—something that is forbidden in some of the communities in the area. Nevertheless, prospective teachers were able to position their placement schools in a general way that started to give them a sense that the school was part of a community, and not a world unto itself. This enabled them to have a baseline of information for the remainder of their placement activities, including the community panel activity described next, as well as for their development of critical reflection through the activities described later in this chapter. It is worth pointing out that if the mapping community asset activity is not coupled with follow-up activities to include voices and lived experiences from members in the community, prospective teachers might stop their analysis at a superficial level that could reinforce the stereotypical deficit view about the community. To combat this danger, plans were made to supplement the information-gathering stage of the project with direct examination of the school's neighborhood using walk-throughs guided by a member of the community who could direct the prospective teachers' attention toward a broader range of assets. For reasons discussed at the end of this chapter, this step was not taken, but we do recommend it for other programs implementing community-based teacher education.

6.6.1 Community Panels

In order to expose prospective teachers to the authentic voices of the communities in which they were placed after mapping out the community asset project, community panels were developed to bring together prospective teachers, in-service teachers, and community members for presentations and conversation. This was usually done in the placement school itself, so that school teachers and community members would have easy access to the event. For example, when Katrina Liu and Arnetha Ball co-taught the methods course in a majority-Latinx field placement school, they organized a community panel that included two parents, an ELL teacher, and the Assistant Principal from the school, a leader from a local organization supporting homeless youth, and a leader from a local organization supporting the LGBTQ+ community. One major purpose of this panel was to demonstrate to the prospective teachers that learning to teach should be built on the wisdom and knowledge of the community, including teachers, parents, and community organizations. Another purpose was to help prospective teachers understand the life experiences of minoritized learners, the dreams and hopes of these students and their families, and the community resources they draw upon to overcome difficulties—all of which differed from the common deficit view that typically results from a lack of engagement with the community. The panel lasted for two hours, each panelist sharing their views of diversity in their specific domain and the knowledge and experiences that they have in working with minoritized populations. For example, the executive director of the partnership for homeless youth shared stories of the challenges homeless youth face as well as stories of strengths and success. The director continued to say:

When children come to school without eating and when they do not know where to go after school, then learning in the class might not be the priority for them, but it does not mean they do not care about learning or they are less capable. We just need to start from where they are.

The ELL teacher pointed out that one reality in the school district was an increasing immigrant population. She emphasized that some newly immigrated students needed time, patience, and support, arguing that teachers should not label them as slow learners simply because of language barriers. The assistant principal shared her philosophy of strength-based teaching: searching for and building upon students' strength. She shared a story about how she found a student's interests and talents in science and used that to motivate them in all of their classes. One Latina parent who was a licensed nurse, a long-term volunteer in the school, shared how she cared about her children's education, modeling the value of education and hard work for her children by volunteering in the school: "When I am not working, I'm here. I care about my children's education and I want to help the teachers." The advice she gave was "Never label my child. Every child has potential."

After the panel, prospective teachers were asked to reflect on what they had learned. They shared that the panel helped them see the importance of building a trust relationship with students and their families. As one White prospective teacher reflected, "The panelists helped me see that racism may not be transparent. You need to get to know the students and find out their life situations." Prospective teachers also believed that the panel discussion helped challenge their prior assumptions about students from minoritized communities. Another White prospective teacher reflected that

Growing up in an upper-middle class household, and now teaching in a similar demographic, has left me with a narrow scope of the challenges some of our students face. I had an "aha" moment when someone on the panel mentioned that some of the kids don't learn because they are in survival mode. They are not retaining the information because they are thinking where their next meal is going to come from, not because they are not smart.

This reflection by the prospective teacher is revealing. They essentially admitted that they had previously assumed that students with learning issues were "not smart," which is a common stereotype of Latinx students, often linked to the idea that their families and communities don't value education. Hearing about food insecurity in the community forced them to rethink that deficit assumption. This is an important step in developing anti-racist approaches to teaching, not just learning about food insecurity but learning about it directly from community members and its consequence on student learning.

6.7   BEGINNING TO ENVISION OTHER WAYS OF BEING AND DOING

Having spent some time considering their own positionality and lived experience, prospective teachers were primed to explore alternative ways to current ways of thinking and living in order to provide an opportunity to challenge prevailing ways of knowing. This is a process of internalization (Ball, 2009; Miller et al., 2020), prompting prospective teachers to advocate for transformation: "Here is how we might change the situation" (Miller et al., 2020, p. 290). The goal was to help them realize that they could replace obsolete, irrational, or oppressive social arrangements with more contemporary, rational, or just alternatives, calling into question the belief that simply because some idea or social structure has existed unchanged for a period of time that it must be right and the best possible arrangement. The stages of critical reflection corresponding to the activities described below were Imaginative Speculation and Reflective Skepticism, together focused on envisioning new ways of being a teacher and doing education, and then examining those imagined innovations with a critical lens, much as is done to assumptions in the previous stages of critical reflection. The primary activity to encourage speculation and skepticism was the *Classroom Discipline Observation and Analysis* project.

6.7.1   *Classroom Discipline Observation and Analysis*

As we have emphasized throughout this book, a key element to preparing White teachers for minoritized student populations is getting them to understand and challenge both toxic habits of mind and patterns of acting. We came to this realization by conducting longitudinal research in which we studied prospective teachers' habits of mind through the analysis of their reflections on their experiences in the classroom—but also by comparing those reflections to what we observed in their classrooms. Ground-truthing preservice teachers' presentation of their reflections, and their description of their classroom experiences, against our own observations taught us just how difficult it is to help them move beyond the presentation of themselves as knowledgeable, accomplished teachers and into authentic critical reflection. We saw again and again that, while some preservice teachers struggled to articulate their experiences and reflect upon them, many more were quite adept at framing those experiences in positive ways and thus avoid authentic reflection. They were then unable to proceed to transformative learning, which requires authentic critical reflection as the basis for transformation.

We further noticed in our research that part of the problem here is prospective teachers were often unable to observe classroom dynamics outside the unconsidered, deficit-based assumptions about minoritized students they absorbed from their own prior experiences with schools, schooling, and teacher education coursework focused on technical aspects of lesson planning and delivery. This not only limited the value of prospective teachers' observations for critical reflection and transformative learning but actually tended to reinforce those deficit views, internalizing "teaching in the shadows" that "produces and supports the present disparities in academic performance among traditionally underserved students" (Hollins, 2019, p. 15). For example, it has long been known that minoritized students—especially Black boys and girls—are disciplined in numbers that far exceed their proportion of the student population, and in the aggregate receive harsher punishments than White students accused of similar infractions of expected behavioral norms (Skiba et al., 2014). Our findings in Chap. 4 documented punishment disparities in detail. The statistics on these disciplinary discrepancies are quite clear, and we have long introduced those statistics through readings to our prospective teachers; prospective teachers from minoritized communities generally respond with recognition and contribute their own experiences with such disciplinary practices, while White prospective teachers tend to respond with shock, outrage, and generalized statements of disbelief—"that's unbelievable!" Such statements of disbelief, while formulaic, also accurately reflect White prospective teachers' lack of critical awareness of discipline disparities and underlying racism. When coupled with a generalized culture in which White individuals and White-serving institutions are afforded "the benefit of the doubt," regarding racism, the result is the preemptive denial of race-based disparities in White prospective teachers' placement schools.

In order to address White prospective teachers' preemptive denial of racial disparities in discipline, all prospective teachers were required to observe and document their mentor teachers' disciplinary actions as well as their own in the classroom throughout one semester to gain an understanding of their students' backgrounds, the classroom rules, and how discipline was conducted on a daily basis. At the beginning of the semester, prospective teachers read articles on school and classroom discipline to learn about the commonly implemented approaches. The discipline approaches prospective teachers observed were consistent with those they read about in the literature, including exclusionary discipline (out-of-school suspension and expulsion) and in-school discipline (office discipline referrals, verbal and non-verbal rebukes, and intensive monitoring). In addition, prospective teachers completed 14 weekly online discussion assignments about their field experiences and assigned readings prior to the weekly face-to-face class. The online discussions were guided by questions covering topics of student diversity and equity, classroom discipline rules and discipline disparity, student assessment and equity, teacher-parent communication, and the like. After gaining basic knowledge about student demographics and discipline rules in their placement classrooms, participants read critical scholarship such as "Preparing teachers for diverse student populations: A Critical Race Theory perspective" (Ladson-Billings, 1999), "A personal case of culturally responsive teaching praxis" (Gay, 2010), "Are we closing the school discipline gap?" (Losen et al., 2015), and "Critical reflection and generativity: Toward a framework of transformative teacher education for diverse Learners" (Liu & Ball, 2019).

Prospective teachers observed the disciplinary actions of their mentor teachers in weeks two to seven. In weeks eight and ten, they documented the disciplinary actions in their placement classroom over one full day, tallying the students (with pseudonyms) who were disciplined that day, their backgrounds, the behavior that caused discipline, and the discipline they received (Table 6.2). Based on the tallies, participants were then asked to comment on the disciplinary actions, whether there could be bias behind the decision, and whether they would act differently if they were the teacher. Finally, participants conducted an end-of-semester reflection on their understanding of student diversity, classroom discipline, and their personal philosophy of teaching diverse students.

Frustratingly, despite evidence of race-based discipline disparities that they themselves collected in their own placement classrooms, White participants tended to approve their mentor teachers' discipline decisions rather than questioning them, asserting that the disciplinary system was race-neutral. For example, Helen documented that her mentor teacher gave a

Table 6.2 Discipline observation tally sheet

Student Name Pseudonym	Student Demographic Backgrounds	Discipline Time & Length	Description of the Infraction	Disciplinary Action
Analysis	Based on your tally and observation, please talk about the patterns of discipline: Do you see some students were disciplined more and harsher than the others? If so, what might be the reasons? If you were the teacher, what would you do?			

warning to a White boy when he played with his marker; she gave another warning 15 minutes later when he talked out loud, and a third when he did not follow instructions when lining up. Helen documented the same mentor teacher giving one verbal warning to a Latinx girl when she talked out loud and then, when she talked a second time, segregating her from the class by sending her to sit by herself. Yet Helen stated in her end-of-semester reflection that her mentor teacher treated all students equally and fairly, "Race, gender, when it comes to discipline it really has no burden of impact"

(Helen's reflection). Dealing with race-evasive behavior of this kind proved difficult; efforts from the instructors to have the participants reevaluate their broad statements in light of the data they collected sometimes provoked a backlash, the participant accusing the instructors of "reverse racism" and giving the course very low student evaluations. Here again we considered bringing community members into the reflective process specifically for the discipline tally project, but for reasons discussed at the end of the chapter, this improvement did not take place.

6.8   DEVELOP, PILOT, AND REFLECT ON ANTI-RACIST TEACHING

The final steps in critical reflection for transformation and generative change are to use the insights produced in the previous stages to develop and pilot transformative problem-solving solutions, gain knowledge and skills from their teacher education community to implement these solutions, and then reflect critically on those actions and their effects on teachers, students, and family in another round of collaborative, community-based reflection. The knowledge generated from implementing the solutions developed in this way leads to generativity (Liu & Ball, 2019): "This is how we changed the situation" and "This is what we learned from action and what comes next?" (Miller et al., 2020, p. 290). To encourage prospective teachers to develop these important critical reflection skills in both stand-alone and collaborative contexts, Liu developed two interrelated sets of prompts keyed to the stages of critical reflection and generative change, one suitable for stimulating collaborative critical reflection in general and the other for a systematic program of collaborative, video-based critical reflection to foster anti-racist teaching.

6.8.1   *Prompting Critical Reflection for Anti-racist Teaching*

The following set of prompts (Table 6.3, adapted from Liu, 2015 and Gao et al., 2019) are designed to encourage prospective teachers to learn to reflect before creating classroom activities, during lesson delivery, and after completing the activities. The prompts are organized according to the stages of critical reflection outlined in Chap. 2 and directed specifically toward developing anti-racist approaches to teaching. They do not, however, need to be followed in a complete sequence. For example, as prospective teachers become more adept at reflection, recognizing the existence of negative

Table 6.3 Prompts for critical reflection for transformative anti-racist teaching

Stage of critical reflection	Prompts
1. Assumption analysis	• What have I learned about my individual students regarding their racial, ethnic, linguistic backgrounds, and their everyday experiences that intersect with race and racism? • What are some essential assumptions I had about my racialized students? • What are some essential assumptions I had about teaching this specific lesson? • Now that I have taught this lesson, what prior assumptions do I find to be wrong and clashed with my students' racialized experiences?
2. Contextual awareness	• What are the social and personal causes of my misassumptions about students' racialized experiences? • Have I observed these misassumptions in my K-12 classrooms as a student? • What negative impact did those misassumptions have on me and my racialized students?
3. Imaginative speculation	• Now that I have identified some misassumptions about students' racialized experiences, what alternative ways could be used to replace my prior teaching?
4. Reflective skepticism	• Why are my prior assumptions about students' racialized experiences problematic? • Why is my prior teaching based on my prior assumptions problematic? • What is the negative impact of my teaching on my students?
5. Community-based learning	• What knowledge and skills do I need to implement my alternative solutions? • What resources are available to implement my alternative solutions? • What can I learn from racially aware parents, mentor teachers, and teacher educators to implement my alternative solutions?
6. Reflection-based action	• What are the assumptions behind the alternative solution(s)? • How am I going to implement the alternatives in my future teaching?
7. Reflection on effects of reflection-based action	• What are the impacts of the alternatives on my racialized students? • Were there wrong assumptions behind the alternative solution(s)? • What further changes should I implement in my future teaching?

Adapted from Liu (2015) and Gao et al. (2019)

assumptions about the students (assumption analysis) and the results of those assumptions on students in the classroom (contextual awareness) can lead directly to reflection-based action. Critical reflection can thus happen in a moment, and need not derail classroom activities and schedules. Indeed, the ability to adapt lessons to individual students on the fly—differentiated instruction in action—is a hallmark of an expert teacher. Using these prompts to encourage critical reflection therefore is an important step for prospective teachers to develop the capabilities of experts. These prompts can be used to support dialogs within the transformative anti-racist teacher education community envisioned at the beginning of this chapter.

6.8.2 Video-Based Collaborative Reflection for Transformative Anti-racist Teaching

Video has been used as a medium for reflection in education since the early 1990s, both for prospective and in-service teachers, and generally as a collaborative project. Hassler and Collins (1993) reported on the Video Portfolio Project of the National Board of Teacher Standards, a collaborative, video-based reflection program for K-12 in-service teachers preparing for the Master Teacher credential. Similarly, Van Zoest (1995) examined the role of video in small groups of preservice teachers engaging in collaborative reflection. By the 2000s, video equipment had become sufficiently available to allow researchers to look beyond the technology itself and consider some of the broader implications for schooling and society. For example, McCurry (2000) argued for video-based reflection to be the springboard for developing critical pedagogy, while Collins et al. (2004) presented video reflection as one component in a complex professional development program in tandem with other technologies supporting role-play, peer review, and other approaches to collaborative development.

Today video-based reflection has become sufficiently common that the ERIC research database contains more than 1500 articles on a range of aspects of the technology, the practice, and the implications for teaching and teacher education. This research provides important findings that helped guide our development of the prompts described below. First, video-based reflection should be conducted under the guidance of an experienced teacher educator to ensure that the collaborative reflection stays on track. Second, prompts and follow-up questions (see the examples below) should work to link theory and practice together, drawing preservice teachers into their students' experiences and counter-narratives with an eye on supporting social justice and educational equity. Third, learning to reflect and to develop transformative practices on the basis of that reflection takes time. It is important not to rush the emergence of authentic reflection, and it is important to return to the practice of reflection as many times as possible. Finally, before implementing video-based reflection, it is vital to work with all stakeholders to ensure that recording and handling the recordings of classroom activities follows the spirit and letter of all relevant ethical guidelines. At the very least, all participants, including school personnel, students, and their families, need to be provided informed consent and an opportunity to opt out of the process. Even if there is no research component to the project, designing the project within the general parameters of human subjects privacy and confidentiality protections is wise. This means placing cameras in locations and with angles that protect student privacy as well as the privacy of any unexpected visitors to the classroom; it also means establishing a secure system to maintain the confidentiality of recordings and any reflection artifacts stemming from those recordings. It should go without saying that no one should post video or descriptions of video on social media—but in today's media-saturated world, this needs to be incorporated into some kind of formal statement signed by everyone with access to the video and related reflection artifacts.

Video-based reflection focuses on the prospective teachers' patterns of acting in the classroom, which in turn can illuminate their habits of mind. Video-based reflection thus presumes a clinical model of teacher education. Our model here also assumes that the clinical model is implemented with a triad of prospective teacher, mentor teacher, and teacher educator. It is always possible to increase the collaborators in the reflection process, such as fellow prospective teachers, school leaders, and community members. However, the triad is the minimum requirement, as the presence of multiple collaborators reduces the opportunities for prospective teachers to avoid reflection. The videos can be recorded during short-term practicum sessions or longer-term student teaching placement, and ideally occur at least twice during the preservice teacher's program so that observations and insights resulting from the reflection can be incorporated into the preservice teacher's instruction.

6.8.3   Prompting Video-Based Reflection
for Anti-racist Teaching

For all the reasons detailed in the preceding sections of this book—especially the need to encourage authentic reflection leading to transformative action rather than performative sidestepping of reflection and transformation—video-based reflection should happen in a non-evaluative environment. To that end, it is important to run the viewing and critiquing process starting with a focus on positive elements—what the prospective teacher has done well, what appears to be innovative, where the students really seem to respond to the lessons—and begin linking concrete events and practices in the classroom to the conceptual and theoretical framework of CRT, critical reflection, and anti-racist teaching. The following prompts for video reflection (Table 6.4, adapted from Liu, 2015 and Gao et al., 2019) attempt to make those linkages in a non-evaluative way. They are designed for use in a series of video reflection sessions, during which all parties should take notes. All video reflection sessions subsequent to the first one should begin with a brief review of notes from the previous session.

Liu (2017) provided multiple examples of the realizations possible with collaborative video reflection. The reader is directed to the particular case

Table 6.4   Prompts for video-based critical reflection for transformative learning

Stage of critical reflection	Prompts
1. Assumption analysis	• What have I learned about my individual students regarding their racial, ethnic and linguistic backgrounds, and their everyday experiences that intersect with race and racism? • What are some essential assumptions I had about my racialized students? • How did I integrate this knowledge into your planning and teaching this lesson?
2. Contextual awareness	• What are the social and personal causes of my misassumptions about students' racialized experiences? • Have I observed these misassumptions in my K-12 classrooms as a student? • What negative impact did those misassumptions have on me as a teacher and my racialized students?

(*continued*)

Table 4.1 (continued)

Stage of critical reflection	Prompts
3. Imaginative Speculation	• How did I create a classroom culture that respects and embraces my students' racialized identities? • Did I treat all the students equitably in classroom discipline, no matter what racial, ethnic, linguistic, and other backgrounds they are from? • Did I provide equal learning opportunities for students to engage deeply in this lesson, especially the racialized students? • What should I do in order to build a more inclusive environment and more equitable opportunities to better support racialized student learning?
4. Reflective skepticism	• Why are my prior assumptions about students' racialized experiences problematic? • How was my teaching in this video based on my prior assumptions problematic? • What is the negative impact of my teaching on my racialized students?
5. Community-based learning	• What knowledge and skills do I need in order to implement my alternative solutions? • What resources are available to implement my alternative solutions? • What can I learn from racially aware parents, mentor teachers, and teacher educators to implement my alternative solutions?
6. Reflection-based action	• What are the assumptions behind the alternative solution(s)? • How am I going to implement the alternatives in my future teaching?
7. Reflection on effects of reflection-based action (after implementation)	• What are the impacts of the alternatives on my racialized students? • Were there wrong assumptions behind the alternative solution(s)? • What further changes should I implement in my future teaching?

Adapted from Liu (2015) and Gao et al. (2019)

of White participant "Anne" (a pseudonym) who initially projected a lack of interest in learning onto one of the African American students in her placement classroom (this episode is described on p. 11). This stereotype changed when Anne learned that the student was battling brain cancer. Subsequently, Anne video recorded some of her classes for collaborative video reflection; her supervisor noted that Anne missed an opportunity to recognize the student's math skills in front of the rest of class, which prompted Anne to realize that she had denied the student an opportunity to be proud, and deprived the other students of the opportunity to learn from her. Had Anne not recorded her lesson and viewed it with other people she would not have recognized her implicit bias nor implemented transformative actions later to recognize and acknowledge the talents and experiences of the African American student.

6.9   WHERE DO WE GO FROM HERE?

In this chapter we have presented the system and procedures that we have been using to prepare White teachers to make a positive difference in teaching students from minoritized communities. We do this by grounding teacher education in the anti-racist insights and procedures of CRT, helping prospective teachers develop skills in critical reflection for transformative learning and generative change, to be able to recognize and modify classroom activities toward anti-racist teaching, and to engage in authentic collaborative reflection using tools such as video-based reflection. We also demonstrate multiple instances in which, even with this carefully designed program, White prospective teachers' transformation remained incomplete, the participants unable to see past their personal experience of dominance and privilege, either when looking for community assets that could be the basis for curriculum and pedagogy, or when observing disciplinary disparities in their placement classrooms.

Finally, we mentioned several activities—mapping community assets and the discipline tally project—that we discussed modifying to improve their ability to encourage the transformation of the preservice teachers' habits of mind and patterns of acting, but were not able to implement these modifications. The reason for this failure is simple but instructive: The program that featured the general methods course in which all these activities took place was restructured to eliminate that course, and the field requirement part of the course was integrated to a classroom management course. We have continued to work with these activities in other courses, but since the elimination of the course, we have not been able to use them all in sequence, and opportunities to collaborate directly with local schools and communities have been severely limited. This points to a problem sadly common in teacher education, the fact that we teacher educators develop programs based on research results and deep theoretical insight, only to have institutional support removed. The reasons for the loss of support vary—internal politics within a department or a university leading to reallocation of duties, or changes in state licensure requirements leading to curricular modifications—but the result is the same: teachers, students, and entire communities rendered disposable (Miller et al., 2021) so that resources can be moved to other priorities.

This institutional setback notwithstanding, we remain committed to anti-racist teaching and our efforts to develop anti-racist teacher education. This is another aspect of the longitudinal aspect of our work: we do not expect the road to educational equity to be without turns and stops. Accordingly, we continue our anti-racist teacher education research and practice by preparing White prospective teachers and prospective teachers of color through community-based approaches. In the final chapter of this book, "The Potential to Transform," we engage in imaginative speculation and reflective skepticism, first learning from the experiences of two prospective teachers of color about how they decriminalize and rehumanize their students, and then re-envisioning one of the key cases of racism toward a student in the classroom discussed in earlier chapters according to the insights provided by the two prospective teachers of color.

References

Ball, A. F. (2009). Toward a theory of generative change in culturally and linguistically complex classrooms. *American Educational Research Journal, 46*(1), 45–72.

Brown, A. L. (2010). Counter-memory and race: An examination of African American scholars' challenges to early twentieth century K-12 historical discourses. *The Journal of Negro Education, 79*(1), 54–65.

Bruna, K. R. (2005). Rethinking resistance in multicultural teacher education: Reflection and miseducation. In D. M. McInerney & S. Van Etten (Eds.), *Focus on curriculum* (pp. 299–326). Information Age Publishing.

Collins, J. L., Cook-Cottone, C. P., Robinson, J. S., & Sullivan, R. R. (2004). Technology and new directions in professional development: Applications of digital video, peer review, and self-reflection. *Journal of Educational Technology Systems, 33*(2), 131–146.

Cox, D., Navarro-Rivera, J., & Jones, R. P. (2016). *Race, religion, and political affiliation of Americans' core social networks.* PRRI. https://www.prri.org/research/poll-race-religion-politics-americans-social-networks/

Crenshaw, K., Gotanda, N., Peller, G., & Thomas, K. (Eds.). (1996). *Critical race theory: The key writings that formed the movement.* New Press.

Dunn, A. H., Dotson, E. K., Ford, J. C., & Roberts, M. A. (2014). "You won't believe what they said in class today:" Professors' reflections on student resistance in multicultural education Courses. *Multicultural Perspectives, 16*(2), 93–98.

Evans-Winters, V. E., & Hines, D. E. (2019). Unmasking white fragility: How whiteness and white student resistance impacts anti-racist education. *Whiteness and Education, 5*(1), 1–16.

Gao, S., Liu, K., & McKinney, M. (2019). Learning formative assessment in the field: Analysis of reflective conversations between preservice teachers and their classroom mentors. *International Journal of Mentoring and Coaching in Education, 8*(3), 197–216.

Gay, G. (2010). A personal case of culturally responsive teaching praxis. In G. Gay (Ed.), *Culturally responsive teaching: Theory, research, and practice* (pp. 249–273). Teachers College Press.

Gonsalves, R. E. (2008). Hysterical blindness and the ideology of denial: Preservice teachers' resistance to multicultural education. *Counterpoints, 319*, 3–27.

Hassler, S. S., & Collins, A. M. (1993). Using collaborative reflection to support changes in classroom practice. Paper presented at the Annual Meeting of the American Educational Research Association, Atlanta, April 12–16, 1993. 30 Retrieved from ERIC Number: ED361330.

Hollins, E. R. (2019). Teaching in the shadow. In E. R. Hollins (Ed.), *Teaching to transform urban schools and communities: Powerful pedagogy in practice* (pp. 1–17). Routledge.

Ladson-Billings, G. (1999). Preparing teachers for diverse student populations: A critical race theory perspective. *Review of Research in Education, 24*(1), 211–247.

Ladson-Billings, G. (2006). From the achievement gap to the education debt: Understanding achievement in U.S. schools. *Educational Researcher, 35*(7), 3–12.

LaDuke, A. E. (2009). Resistance and renegotiation: Preservice teacher interactions with and reactions to multicultural education course content. *Multicultural Education, 16*(3), 37–44.

Liu, K. (2015). Critical reflection as a framework for transformative learning in teacher education. *Educational Review, 67*(2), 135–157.

Liu, K. (2017). Creating a dialogic space for prospective teacher critical reflection and transformative learning. *Reflective Practice, 18*(6), 805–820.

Liu, K. (2020). *Critical reflection for transformative learning.* Springer.

Liu, K., & Ball, A. F. (2019). Critical reflection and generativity: Toward a framework of transformative teacher education for diverse learners. *Review of Research in Education, 43*(1), 68–105.

Liu, K., Miller, R., & Ball, A. F. (2023). Teacher education for diverse learners. In R. J. Tierney, F. Rizvi, & K. Erkican (Eds.), *International Encyclopedia of Education, vol. 5* (pp. 356–367). Elsevier.

Losen, D. J., Hodson, C. L., Keith, M. A., II, Morrison, K., & Belway, S. (2015). *Are we closing the school discipline gap?* UCLA Center for Civil Rights Remedies. https://escholarship.org/content/qt2t36g571/qt2t36g571.pdf

Matias, C. (2018). *Feeling White: Whiteness, emotionality, and education.* Brill.

156   K. LIU ET AL.

McCurry, D. S. (2000). Technology for critical pedagogy: Beyond self-reflection with video. In: Society for Information Technology & Teacher Education International Conference: Proceedings of SITE 2000 (11th, San Diego, February 8–12, 2000), 7 pp. Retrieved from ERIC Number: ED444458.

McIntosh, P. (1989). White privilege: Unpacking the invisible knapsack. *Peace and Freedom Magazine*, July/August, 10–12. Reprinted with McIntosh 2010 by the National SEED Project on Inclusive Curriculum, Wellesley College. https://nationalseedproject.org/images/documents/Knapsack_plus_Notes-Peggy_McIntosh.pdf

McIntosh, P. (2010). Some notes for facilitators. Printed with McIntosh 1989 by the National SEED Project on Inclusive Curriculum, Wellesley College. https://nationalseedproject.org/images/documents/Knapsack_plus_Notes-Peggy_McIntosh.pdf

Miller, R., Liu, K., & Ball, A. F. (2020). Critical counter-narrative as transformative methodology for educational equity. *Review of Research in Education, 44*(1), 269–300.

Miller, R., Liu, K., & Ball, A. F. (2021). After the virus: Disaster capitalism, digital inequity, and transformative education for the future of schooling. *Education and Urban Society, 55*(5), 533–554.

Milner, H. R. (2010). *Start where you are, but don't stay there: Understanding diversity, opportunity gaps, and teaching in today's classrooms.* Harvard Education Press.

Milner, H. R. (2023). *The race card: Leading the fight for truth in America's schools.* Corwin.

Skiba, R. J., Arredondo, M. I., & Williams, N. T. (2014). More than a metaphor: The contribution of exclusionary discipline to a school-to-prison pipeline. *Equity & Excellence in Education, 47*(4), 546–564.

Van Zoest, L. R. (1995). The impact of small-group discussion on preservice teachers' observations and reflections. Paper presented at the Annual Meeting of the American Educational Research Association, San Francisco, April 18–22, 1995. 34 pp. Retrieved from ERIC Number: ED385491.

CHAPTER 7

The Potential to Achieve

Although the focus of this book is on preparing White prospective teachers to teach minoritized students and we did not intend to compare White prospective teachers' habits of mind and patterns of acting with those of prospective teachers from minoritized communities, we would like to provide some examples of what habits of mind and patterns of acting can be like when prospective teachers are more racially aware and able to implement humanizing and decriminalizing teaching. We first present the stories of two prospective teachers of color from minoritized communities who were part of the communities where they taught. These teachers, also students in our teacher education programs, came into our programs with access to their community funds of knowledge. However, as Rios-Aguilar and Kiyama (2012) demonstrated, access to community funds of knowledge does not automatically translate into the ability to mobilize those funds of knowledge for transformative change. Rather, prospective teachers of color need to understand how their racialized experiences are situated in the larger system of white privilege and white supremacy. They also need the opportunity to reflect on their own funds of knowledge so that they can mobilize them in the process of teaching and supporting minoritized students, as demonstrated in Chap. 6, through learning from counter-narratives and dialogue with other prospective teachers of color. The two teachers of color we discuss in this chapter learned these key skills as a result of their engagement with the same training in anti-racist

K. Liu et al., *Preparing White Teachers for Anti-Racist Education*, https://doi.org/10.1007/978-3-031-73534-9_7

teaching as the White prospective teachers discussed in this book. We use the stories of these two teachers of color for three reasons. First, to provide positive examples of the links that are possible (but not guaranteed) between community funds of knowledge and educational equity. Second, to underscore the fact that the theories and practices described in this book are not just intended for White preservice teachers. Third, to draw lessons for White teachers in order to encourage their engagement with community funds of knowledge. We end the chapter and the book by reimagining key episodes of toxic habits of mind and patterns of acting discussed earlier in the book, intending to show how, with the benefit of anti-racist teacher education, the oppressed experiences of the children at the center of those episodes could have been transformed.

7.1   Sofia and Jevon

Sofia, who is Latina, was one of the prospective teachers in Desert View University. She grew up in an urban community in the Southwest; more than 90% of the students in the elementary school Sofia attended were from a very stable local Latinx community. Sofia grew up in a single-mother family, her mom first working as a cleaner and then building her own small cleaning business. During the Privilege Race, Sofia, like Jevon, was not able to move many steps forward. However, she shared that although her mom was not able to speak much English she worked very hard to support Sofia's education. She remembered many times her mom brought her along on cleaning jobs, but always making sure she completed her homework on time. What she learned from her mom is to be hardworking and never give up. Sofia's mom always told her that even though they had challenges such as language barriers, they could turn those challenges into assets and strengths. Sofia never had a Latinx teacher throughout her K-12 education and therefore never thought she could become a teacher. She picked law school to become a lawyer, and worked in a law firm for nine years before deciding to join the alternative route to teaching program at Desert View University. She also earned a master's degree in history, but noted that most of her history courses and readings presented history from a White perspective. Nevertheless, through critical readings and course activities as described in Chap. 6, Sofia started to make connections between her lived experiences and the history and current realities of students like her. In an interview, Sofia stated:

The discussions in this course really opened up a whole world for me. I always thought about diversity, but not until in the course when we talked about diversity from an asset point of view and the problem of the student-teacher diversity gap in schools, that I feel what I thought and believed before is confirmed. For example, I was never taught by a teacher like me so when I was little, I wondered why but I never thought I could be a teacher. Now I see the problem. I started to open up and believe that it is important to share my stories and history, instead of always listening to other people's perspectives. I became more comfortable to defend my perspectives for the purpose of defending students who share my backgrounds, struggles, and experiences.

Sofia and her mom have lived in the community since she was little and built great connections with other families in the community, who babysat Sofia when her mom was busy and celebrated both her college matriculation and her graduation with gifts and laughter. Sofia said she literally knew every single family in the community because it was HER community. Therefore, when she started her field experience in the teacher education program, she requested student teaching in the elementary school she attended: Her dream was to teach in this school to pay back to her community. During her student teaching, her connection with the community enabled her to build trust relationships with the students immediately. Right after she completed her student teaching, her dream came true: She was offered the job to teach first grade in her school.

Jevon is a Black male prospective teacher at Desert View University. His parents absent, he was raised by his grandparents. Jevon remembered that, during K-12 schooling, he was always told that he was a "trouble-maker" and he accepted that label. As discussed in Chap. 6, Jevon shared during the privilege race activity that after high school he was jailed for six months without having committed any crime. He and his friends were in a car and stopped by the police; he was arrested because he wore clothes similar to those of a suspect who conducted a robbery. Later he learned that, while he was in jail, the real suspect was caught but the police still did not release him for months. After he got out of jail, he studied hard and applied for college with the support of some community members. During college he coached many after-school programs, and after college graduation, he worked as a substitute teacher for a few years before joining the teacher education program at the Desert View University. When he participated in the study, he was simultaneously in the program and teaching physical education and computer science at a local charter school.

7.2   Asset-Based Habits of Mind

Both Sofia and Jevon recounted experiences of spirit murder (Bryan, 2021) and racial battle fatigue (Smith, 2004) due to racial discrimination and oppression they encountered in their education and work. They experienced racial violence, typically organized via deficit stereotypes, such as being a dangerous, disrespectful, and defiant Black boy (Jevon), and a lazy, language deficient, Mexican girl uninterested in education (Sofia). At the same time, their own counter-narratives of family and community support, resilience, and hard work enabled them to see students like themselves from an asset point of view. Their experiences of school-based trauma (Duane, 2023) gave them a critical consciousness of how educational inequity operates and urged them to enter education in order to make a difference for the next generation of minoritized students. As Sofia stated in an interview:

> My mom showed me the family value of hard work and my neighbors demonstrated to me community collaboration and support. I know all the neighborhood and the shops around. They live down the street. Some of the families have lived in the neighborhood for a long time and they took a sense of pride. They take care of the community and they all care genuinely about their children's education. I am always sad and also angry when we hear people say Mexicans don't care about education.

Jevon's racialized experience of schools and schooling similarly informed him of institutional racism and inequity. He had a keen understanding of the struggles of kids like himself and he was dedicated to supporting them. After the Privilege Race activity, Jevon reflected that:

> I was always told I was the trouble maker, the clown kid. I believed it as a kid. Like a lot of kids of color, I got punished constantly. Now I understand the system better. I'm not less intelligent, I'm not less hardworking. I graduated from high school, I graduated from college, and I'm here today. I want to show my kids that they have tal-

ents and they have the potential to succeed. I am here to tell them they can do it and I am here to provide them the support. (Jevon, Class Discussion)

One comment both Sophia and Jevon constantly made with reference to their students was: "I see myself in them. I don't want them to experience racism as I did."

7.3   Humanizing and Decriminalizing Patterns of Acting

Classroom observations demonstrated that Sofia and Jevon did not just stop at pledging commitment to equity and justice. Instead, they actively integrated humanizing and decriminalizing actions in their practices. During one observation, Sofia was teaching first grade that semester. All the students were from her Latinx community. When the students had just come in from science, Sophia welcomed them back to class, greeting several of the students in Spanish. The students she greeted in Spanish were very excited to respond in Spanish as well. Later, in an interview, one of us asked what Sofia was talking about with the students and Sofia said she was asking the two boys about their older sisters, whom she had had in class the previous year. She wanted to know how they were doing this year. During student recess, Sofia told me that one of her students, Ayana, shared with her proudly that she was the first person in her family to speak English and she was proud of the student. When the researcher commented that she spoke Spanish with them in class, Sofia responded very positively,

Oh yes definitely! I had two students, one from Honduras, one from Tijuana, and they were in my class because they don't speak English. I speak Spanish with them and help explain in English too. So they learned quickly. One month later, they moved up. Their ability is there, just the language took them a little time to get used to.

During her teaching, Sofia made sure to interact with each student individually, giving equal attention to them. Strikingly, she never needed to raise her voice in class, and never called out specific students for policing purposes as described in Chap. 4. She always used positive reinforcement and encouragement such as "I'll see which team are good listeners… I like how Laila and Angela are working on their whiteboard… Diego, good job! You are showing active listening… Gabriela, good job, I'm very proud of you!" After the lesson, before leaving for lunch, the students cleaned up the floor, putting chairs on top of the tables. In just a couple of minutes the classroom was tidy and clean. They did all this happily and without much prompting from Sofia. While Katrina was waiting for the students to return from lunch, she saw one Latino boy returning early. He quickly picked up a couple of pairs of headphones from a table and placed them on a rack. She asked the student why he did this. He responded that he realized the headphones were still out, and he wanted to make sure they were put away. Was he assigned to do that? The boy smiled, and said "No, I just want to make sure our room stays nice." From this small incident we see that the child used the term "our room," asserting ownership and belonging. He felt like part of the class and wanted to make the classroom a pleasant space for learning.

Sofia's attitude toward her students, her ability to bond with them through language and an appeal to shared experience, contrasts sharply with the example of Craig described in Chap. 4. Also placed in a majority-Latinx school, Craig's commitment to Whiteness meant that he operated from a deficit viewpoint, making no effort to see the students as regular human beings, but as troublemakers to be dealt with using surveillance, policing, and body controlling.

Jevon also drew upon his own experience as a "troublemaker" in school to work with his students. During one observation, Jevon was talking to a Black girl who seemed to be upset. Jevon took her aside and said:

> Yes I understand you are upset because you did not initiate the conflict, but you were responsible for your own behavior. This is a lesson to learn and you need to take the responsibility. I believe you can shape it up. You have great potential and I have confidence in you. If you need to be alone for a minute, you can do it. Take a deep breath and come back when you feel better. (Jevon observation)

The student was asked to have a behavior report because she had some problems with another two students: The other two students said mean things to her and then she pushed them. Jevon observed that she played a role in this issue but he wanted to give her the high expectation that she can move on.

I want to make sure they understand they are sometimes responsible for their behaviors but it does not mean they have no future. I am tough with them but I'm also the person here to support them and put an arm around them to give them the confirmation. (Jevon interview)

Counter-narratives of Sofia and Jevon's decriminalizing teaching featured humanizing patterns of acting, including acknowledging and rewarding excellence, honoring the social and emotional needs of children of color, using respectful words, embracing cultural heritages, and enacting equitable treatment during conflicts. Some of these patterns of acting are congruent with Basile's (2021) categorization of decriminalizing practices in elementary schools such as "assuming brilliance," maintaining "highly respectful interactions," "repairing" the racial injuries, and employing "positive reframing" (234). The transformative praxis of Sofia and Jevon embraced the cultural practices and identities of their students of color, and worked to restore the humanity of the children and families of color. The asset-based habits of mind and humanizing and decriminalizing patterns of acting by Sofia and Jevon highlight the importance of recruiting, supporting, and retaining teachers of color (Bryan, 2021; Gist, 2017; Gist et al., 2019; Kohli, 2014; Liu & Ball, 2019; Philip, 2010; Villegas & Irvine, 2010) and supporting their experience-based praxis in order to begin dismantling the multigenerational violence against minoritized students. These findings also bring us hope that when White prospective teachers become racially aware, are able to recognize and understand the counter-narratives of prospective teachers of color as well as those of their students, and are able to implement anti-racist praxis based on these new habits of mind, children from minoritized communities will stop suffering from the multigenerational violence and spirit murder documented in Chaps. 3 and 4. To suggest how that might happen, we conclude this book by revisiting Jamal's experiences, asking: What if his teachers were equipped with asset-based habits of mind and humanizing and decriminalizing patterns of acting?

7.4   Reimagining Humanizing and Decriminalization: The Case of Jamal, Reconsidered

Now let's consider the anti-racist teaching approaches Sofia and Jevon took toward their students, decriminalizing and rehumanizing them, as a guide to how White prospective teachers can avoid reinscribing racism in their teaching practice. In a theorization of counter-narrative as praxis, Miller et al. (2020) identified three common approaches to counter-narrative:

1. *Whole narrative*, which elicits entire counter-narratives from research participants;
2. *Narrative factors*, in which researchers collect data of various types from participants to construct counter-narratives; and
3. *Composite*, in which the researchers create characters based on narrative factors.

We return to the case of Jamal who, as described in Chaps. 3 and 4, was treated like a criminal by the White prospective teacher Abby and the White mentor teacher and, ultimately, by his White classmates as well. Here we engage in counterfactual reimagination by creating composite characters of Jamal, Abby, and Abby's mentor teacher using narrative factors gleaned from the cases of Sofia and Jevon to decriminalize Jamal's experiences and rehumanize his treatment in the classroom. In the reimagined reality, Abby writes in her ePortfolio reflection that Jamal is not engaged in learning and being defiant and her university supervisor reads her reflection and notes down some prompting questions. With this information in mind, during a post-teaching triad meeting with Abby and her mentor teacher, the university supervisor prompts Abby to think of possible reasons for the behaviors Abby observed. The supervisor encourages Abby to get to know Jamal since he is new to the class. One simple approach is to send a welcome letter for Jamal to take home to his parents. Abby and her mentor teacher agree and take immediate action. They write a letter to extend their warm welcome to not only Jamal but also to the family and the community, and invite the parents to drop in at their convenience to know about the class and the school. More importantly, the letter states that as teachers, they would like to learn from the parents about Jamal's interests and needs so that they could support him fully.

Upon receiving this warm welcome letter, Jamal's parents schedule a visit. During the meeting, Abby and her mentor teacher listen to the parents carefully. They learn that, although Jamal was born in the United States, both parents are from Niger; when Jamal was three years old, they returned to Niger to conduct research and teach. After a few years they were hired by Clear Water University as faculty, which is how Jamal became a student in the local elementary school. The parents share that Jamal speaks fluent English but had no formal schooling experience in the United States prior to settling in Clear Water and entering first grade. He might need a little more time to get familiar with the routines and instructions but he is a very friendly boy and always eager to learn. He is good at math and loves cars. He is very good at drawing pictures of all kinds of cars, and always eager to share his knowledge about cars.

During this meeting, in addition to learning about Jamal and his family, Abby and her mentor teacher provide Jamal's parents with an introduction package that includes information about the classroom routines, daily schedules, and the teachers' contact information. Also, after knowing Jamal's parents both teach at Clear Water University, Abby is excited to explain that she is a student teacher from the Curriculum and Instruction Department in the same university. Abby's mentor teacher follows up by extending a warm invitation for future guest-speaking on topics in their area of expertise to the students. Jamal's parents accept this invitation and also explain that they are happy to welcome Jamal's classmates to tour their lab on the university campus. This meeting not only helps build mutual respect and trust between Jamal's parents and Abby and the mentor teacher but also lays the foundation for future teacher-parent collaboration based on an asset-based habit of mind from the side of Jamal's teachers. After the meeting, Abby reflects that

> I now totally understand why Jamal didn't seem to be engaged. He needs just a little more time to feel comfortable with the new environment. I realized we used harsh tones toward him and that is why he was resistant. I also realized that I assumed that he was not willing to learn based on what I saw on the surface level which was problematic.

With good knowledge of Jamal's background and interests, Abby does not operate from a deficit standpoint. She does not think of Jamal as someone who is lazy, unteachable, defiant, violent, and dangerous, but she does realize that he is not completely familiar with classroom routines yet. So, when drilling the students in reading the time on a clock, Abby knows that Jamal may not realize what comes next. When he finishes reading the time she tells him "Good—you're done here! Please line up at the door to go to music." Jamal goes to the door rather than being left standing in the middle of the room, so the mentor teacher isn't concerned that he hadn't done reading the time yet. If the mentor teacher does ask why Jamal is at the door, Abby will quickly respond that he finished the task so he's ready to go to music. Moreover, with Jamal's position at the door established by Abby's instruction, there is no opening for his White classmates to interrogate him and no reason for the mentor teacher to send him back to read the clock again. He is already there when the two White boys arrive, so the conflict over line position doesn't happen, which means that Abby and the mentor teacher do not grab Jamal and take him out of the room. In any case, if a conflict does arise, Abby and the mentor teacher carefully listen to both Jamal and the two White boys before acting, and make clear to both parties that the White children are not authorized to police their classmates.

When Abby observes Jamal having trouble with his Nook Book, she walks over, kneels down next to him, and helps him get it working, just as she did for the White girl. Because Abby and her mentor teacher model their support and welcoming manner for all students, the rest of the class members are eager to provide a hand, so when Jamal sits between the two White boys, the three of them play math games on the Nook Book together until shifting to the next choice. During this round, the three boys choose to do art. Abby comes over to their table, saying "Jamal, you are a great artist and I love the cars you drew before. Would you like to teach your friends how to draw a car?" Jamal happily nods and the two White boys are excited to get paper and crayons. Jamal is very patient to teach them step by step. At the end of this activity, each boy draws a beautiful car and Abby posts them on the wall to demonstrate their great work. A few weeks into the semester, Jamal has become very familiar with the classroom routines and he has made friends in class. He is always eager to go to school.

In the middle of the semester, Jamal's parents follow through on their offer to collaborate with Abby and her mentor teacher, and come to their class to talk about sandhill cranes, which nest in the Clear Water area. They show pictures and videos of the birds, explain to the class about their habitat, food, and migration patterns, and discuss research they themselves have conducted on cranes at a nearby bird sanctuary. The presentation ends with an explanation of a pen-pal project done by the Crane Foundation in the state that Jamal's parents are part of, connecting students in schools near the bird sanctuary with students in South America, where the cranes migrate to. The students finish the day drawing pictures of the cranes. They are very engaged, especially Jamal, whose eyes sparkle with pride. After the guest talk, Jamal's parents and Abby's mentor teacher also talk about arranging a field trip to their lab before the end of the semester;

Jamal's parents promise to link his teacher to the Crane Foundation for potential pen pal projects in the future.

Seeing Abby's growth and success in building a trust relationship with Jamal and his family, Abby's university supervisor invites her and her mentor teacher to share their experiences at a community panel that the supervisor organizes for prospective teachers at Clear Water University. The community panel includes Jamal's parents, Abby, Abby's mentor teacher, another two Latinx parent volunteers from the local community, and a social worker. During the panel, the parents share their stories about their children, their family values, and their dedication to their children's education. Abby and her mentor teacher shared the stories how they first did not know Jamal enough to support him and how they have built great connections with Jamal's parents. They are proud to share that this trust relationship brings opportunities for collaboration to better teach all the students in the classroom. A parent volunteer comments:

> I appreciate you all taking the time to know about our kids and treat them just like normal kids without labeling them. When I was in elementary school, my teachers never asked me about my family background. I was born in the United States and I speak English but they put me in ELL classes based on my name and how I look. I am glad my children don't need to suffer from the same treatment.

The community panel concludes with more ideas for strengthening the school, university, and community connections. These conversations with real life stories provide a new lens for prospective teachers to understand supporting students from the minoritized communities. The next step for teacher educators at Clear Water University is to continue creating opportunities for prospective teachers to deepen their understanding of students, families, and communities and more importantly, support them to implement transformative anti-racist teaching in their real-classroom teaching.

7.5   Postscript: A Transformative and Generative Community of Teacher Education

The basic goal of this book, and of our work as teacher educators, is to reshape teacher education so that it no longer produces teachers who will continue the intergenerational heritage of violence and trauma perpetuated by racialized systems and practices of education. We have focused on White teachers for this book, in no small part because they constitute the bulk of the teacher corps in the United States, and given how slow the profession has been to diversify even before right-wing attacks on affirmative action and DEI practices, White hegemony among educators is unlikely to change anytime soon. This fact does not mean that recruiting, retaining, and promoting teachers from minoritized communities is not important. Indeed, it is highly unlikely that White supremacy in education will end without a major shift in the demographics of the teacher corps. It is important, therefore, to continue and redouble efforts to diversify the teacher workforce.

Even if the demographics of the teacher corps were to shift overnight, however, we would still argue for restructuring teacher education to be community based, equity focused, and transformative in nature, centering the goal of dismantling racism in teaching and teacher education. By integrating the transformative teacher education framework in a community of school teachers, prospective teachers, university teacher educators, and parents and community members (See Fig. 6.2 in Chap. 6), as reimagined in the story above, we can prepare a new generation of anti-racist teachers. As the prospective teachers become in-service teachers, they continue to work with the community to generate new knowledge (Ball, 2009) to support colleagues and mentor prospective teachers to become transformative intellectuals (Giroux, 1988) and anti-racist educators. The ultimate goal of this transformative and generative change (Ball, 2009; Liu & Ball, 2019) is a humanizing and decriminalizing educational experience for all students, especially those who have been minoritized by society and schooling for whatever reason. This is a potential to achieve, and we believe the steps we have laid out in this book provide a path to realize that potential.

References

Ball, A. F. (2009). Toward a theory of generative change in culturally and linguistically complex classrooms. *American Educational Research Journal, 46*(1), 45–72.

Basile, V. (2021). Decriminalizing practices: Disrupting punitive-based racial oppression of boys of color in elementary school classrooms. *International Journal of Qualitative Studies in Education, 34*(3), 228–242.

Bryan, N. (2021). *Toward a BlackBoyCrit pedagogy: Black boys, male Teachers, and early childhood classroom practices*. Routledge.

Duane, A. (2023). School-based trauma: A scoping review. *Journal of Trauma Studies in Education, 2*(2), 102–124.

Giroux, H. (1988). *Teachers as intellectuals: Toward a critical pedagogy of learning*. Bergin & Garvey.

Gist, C. D. (2017). Voices of aspiring teachers of color: Unraveling the double bind in teacher education. *Urban Education, 52*(8), 927–956.

Gist, C. D., Bianco, M., & Lynn, M. (2019). Examining grow your own programs across the teacher development continuum: Mining research on teachers of color and nontraditional Educator pipelines. *Journal of Teacher Education, 70*(1), 13–25.

Kohli, R. (2014). Unpacking internalized racism: Teachers of color striving for racially just classrooms. *Race Ethnicity and Education, 17*(3), 367–387.

Liu, K., & Ball, A. (2019). Critical reflection and generativity: Toward a framework of transformative teacher education for diverse learners. *Review of Research in Education, 43*, 68–105.

Miller, R., Liu, K., & Ball, A. (2020). Critical counter-narrative as transformative methodology for educational equity. *Review of Research in Education, 44*(1), 269–300.

Philip, T. M. (2010). Moving beyond our progressive lenses: Recognizing and building on the strengths of teachers of color. *Journal of Teacher Education, 62*(4), 356–366.

Rios-Aguilar, C., & Kiyama, J. M. (2012). Funds of knowledge: An approach to studying Latino(a) students' transition to college. *Journal of Latinos and Education, 11*, 2–16.

Smith, W. A. (2004). Black faculty coping with racial battle fatigue: The campus racial climate in a post-civil rights era. In D. Cleveland (Ed.), *A long way to go: Conversations about race by African American faculty and graduate students* (pp. 171–190). Peter Lang.

Villegas, A. M., & Irvine, J. J. (2010). Diversifying the teaching force: An examination of major arguments. *The Urban Review, 42*, 175–192.

INDEX

© The Author(s), under exclusive license to Springer Nature
Switzerland AG 2024
K. Liu et al., *Preparing White Teachers for Anti-Racist Education*,
https://doi.org/10.1007/978-3-031-73534-9

GPSR Compliance

The European Union's (EU) General Product Safety Regulation (GPSR) is a set of rules that requires consumer products to be safe and our obligations to ensure this.

If you have any concerns about our products, you can contact us on ProductSafety@springernature.com

In case Publisher is established outside the EU, the EU authorized representative is:

Springer Nature Customer Service Center GmbH
Europaplatz 3
69115 Heidelberg, Germany

The manufacturer's authorised representative in the EU is Springer
Nature Customer Service Centre GmbH, Europaplatz 3, 69115 Heidelberg,
Germany. If you have any concerns regarding our products, please
contact ProductSafety@springernature.com

Printed and bound by CPI Group (UK) Ltd, Croydon, CR0 4YY
29/04/2026
02099538-0001